imensions of United States-Mexican Relations

olume 4

he Drug Connection
1 U.S.-Mexican Relations

Dimensions of United States-Mexican Relations

a series

Volume 1.   *Images of Mexico in the United States*, edited by John H. Coatsworth and Carlos Rico, with contributions from Christine E. Contee, John Bailey, Carlos E. Cortés, and Gerald Greenfield.

Volume 2.   *The Economics of Interdependence: Mexico and the United States*, edited by William Glade and Cassio Luiselli, with contributions from Barry Bosworth, Francisco Gil Díaz, Rosario Green, Luis Bravo Aguilera, Guy Erb, Joseph Greenwald, Manuel Armendáriz, and B. Timothy Bennett.

Volume 3.   *Mexican Migration to the United States: Origins, Consequences, and Policy Options*, edited by Wayne Cornelius and Jorge Bustamante, with contributions from Wayne Cornelius, Manuel García y Griego, Marta Tienda, Kitty Calavita, and Jorge Bustamante.

Volume 4.   *The Drug Connection in U.S.-Mexican Relations*, edited by Marta Tienda and Guadalupe González, with contributions from Ann J. Blanken, Miguel Ruiz-Cabañas I., Richard B. Craig, and Samuel I. del Villar.

Volume 5.   *Foreign Policy in U.S.-Mexican Relations*, edited by Rosario Green and Peter H. Smith, with contributions from Guadalupe González, Lars Schoultz, Jorge Chabat, Carlos Rico, Cathryn L. Thorup, Claude Heller, and William H. Luers.

Series editors:
Rosario Green and Peter H. Smith

The Drug Connection in U.S.-Mexican Relations

edited by
Guadalupe González and Marta Tienda

Dimensions of U.S.-Mexican Relations, Volume 4
papers prepared for the
Bilateral Commission on the Future of United States-Mexican Relations

Published by the
Center for U.S.-Mexican Studies
University of California, San Diego
1989

ISBN # 0-935391-94-0

Table of Contents

SECTION I

THE TWO FACES OF THE PROBLEM

SECTION II

POLICIES AND POLICY ALTERNATIVES

Dimensions of United States-Mexican Relations: Series Introduction

Rosario Green and Peter H. Smith

This volume is part of a five-volume series, *Dimensions of United States-Mexican Relations,* consisting of selected background papers originally prepared for the use of the Bilateral Commission on the Future of United States-Mexican Relations.

Appreciation of the series must begin with an understanding of its origin. The Bilateral Commission was formed in 1986 as an independent, privately funded group of prominent citizens who were seeking to make a contribution to the improvement of U.S.-Mexican relations. Early in its deliberations the Commission agreed to produce a book-length report in time for consideration by incoming presidents to be elected in 1988.

With a two-year schedule, the Commission decided to seek the opinions of expert analysts on a variety of issues—specifically, on economics (including debt, trade, and investment), migration, drugs, foreign policy, and cultural relations. In addition, of course, Commissioners read a great deal of already published material and heard testimony from numerous government officials in both Mexico and the United States.

As staff directors for the Commission, the two of us assumed responsibility for coordination of the research activity. With the assistance of an Academic Committee,[1] we organized an intensive series of workshops and solicited papers from leading experts on each of these broad topics.

Our principal purpose was to provide the Commission with a broad range of informed perspectives on key issues in U.S.-Mexican relations. We wanted to introduce its members to the terms of current debates, rather than buttress conventional wisdoms; we sought to acquaint them with the broadest possible range of policy alternatives, rather than bias the discussion in favor of any particular view.

As a result, many Commissioners do not agree with the opinions expressed in these papers—just as some of the authors may disagree with parts of the Commission's report, published in English as *The Challenge of Interdependence: Mexico and the United States* (University Press of America, 1988).[2]

Accordingly, the publication of this series does not necessarily represent the viewpoints of the Commission or its members, and the papers herein do not simply provide supporting documentation for positions and recommendations of the Commission. The *Dimensions of United States-Mexican Relations* series represents an outgrowth of the same initiative that resulted in the Commission's report, but in other senses it is separate from it.

As we developed our research program on behalf of the Bilateral Commission, we nonetheless sought to make useful contributions to scholarly discourse on U.S.-Mexican relations. In this regard we had three goals:

One was to encourage the application of *comparative perspectives* to the study of U.S.-Mexican relations. Much of the work in this field has tended to concentrate on properties of the bilateral relationship alone and to assume, and often to assert, that the U.S.-Mexican connection has been "unique." It goes without saying, however, that you cannot determine the uniqueness of a relationship without comparing it to others. This we invited our authors to do.

Second was to encourage appropriate *attention to the United States*. We believe that much of the literature tends to concentrate

---

[1]The members were: Jorge Bustamante, John Coatsworth, Wayne Cornelius, William Glade, Guadalupe González, Cassio Luiselli, Carlos Rico, and Marta Tienda.
[2]The Spanish-language version appeared under the title *El desafío de la interdependencia: México y Estados Unidos* (Mexico: Fondo de Cultura Económica, 1988).

too much on Mexico, on Mexico's problems, and on Mexican contributions to the state of the relationship. We wanted to correct that
imbalance and, at the same time, to promote the study of the United
States by Mexican students and scholars.[3]

Third was to encourage analysts to spell out the *policy
implications* of their work. Academic investigation and primary
research have enormous value, of course, but we hoped to provide
an opportunity for scholars to speak as directly as possible to the
policy-making community. Accordingly, we asked each contribu-
tor to provide practical policy recommendations; in addition, we
obtained some papers from specialists with policy experience and
authority.

With such criteria in mind we solicited and obtained forty-eight
papers that were presented at about a dozen workshops in 1987
and early 1988.[4] These presentations proved to be of great use to
the Bilateral Commission. With the aid of the Academic Committee, we then defined a set of topics for the volumes in this series.
We selected papers for inclusion in the series primarily on the basis
of their relationship to these particular subjects. This led us,
regrettably, to exclude many fine papers from this collection. But
our purpose has been to produce anthologies with thematic coher-
ence as well as substantive originality, and we hope to have
achieved that goal.

We conclude with an expression of thanks to all of our authors,
especially to those whose papers are not in these volumes; to
members of the Commission and its co-chairmen, Hugo Margáin
and William D. Rogers; to our colleagues on the Academic
Committee; to officers at the Ford Foundation who made possible
this enterprise. Sandra del Castillo, Lee Dewey, Will Heller,
Blanca Salgado, Gerardo Santos, and Arturo Sarukhan all made
invaluable contributions to the editing and production of these
volumes; to them our heartfelt gratitude.

Mexico City

La Jolla

---

[3]Indeed, one of the most alarming findings of the Commission relates to the decline
of U.S. studies in Mexico. See *Challenge*, ch. 6.
[4]A complete listing of all papers appears in Appendix II of the Commission's report,
The Challenge of Interdependence. Papers not included in this series may be published elsewhere and are available upon request; please send written inquiries to
the U.S. Office of the Bilateral Commission, Institute of the Americas, 10111 North
Torrey Pines Road, La Jolla, CA 92037.

1

The Drug Connection in U.S.-Mexican Relations: Introduction

Guadalupe González González

In recent years drug traffic has become a constant source of tension between Mexico and the United States. In the dynamic relationship between the two countries, old problems remain as new issues and circumstances arise—including the topic of drugs, perhaps the most disruptive of them all. The overtly political treatment of the drug problem, in all its rhetorical inadequacy, has distorted the order of priorities on the United States-Mexican negotiating agenda and thus contributed to a general deterioration of the bilateral relationship.

The essays in this volume are part of a collective effort to undertake a systematic and objective study of the increasingly complex problem of drugs in the context of U.S.-Mexican relations. The purpose of this introductory essay is to trace the development of new features in the age-old problem of drug abuse and trafficking.

NEW DIMENSIONS TO AN OLD PROBLEM

Although the question of drug traffic and drug control has a long history in U.S.-Mexican relations, the relative importance of the problem—as source of dispute or basis for cooperation—has varied significantly over the past seventy years. It assumed a central place on the bilateral agenda when growing illicit drug use in postwar industrialized societies spurred the internationalization of the drug market and the consolidation of international production networks under the control of organized crime. At one point the drug problem was transformed from a routine topic with modest importance into an explosive, highly visible, political issue; at another it went from being a shining example of bilateral cooperation to a symbol of mutual distrust and chronic lack of communication.

After Operation Intercept I, in 1969, the United States and Mexico decided to establish a plan for permanent cooperation on drug control. Conflict from that first operation nonetheless meant that the bases for bilateral discussion of the drug trafficking issue remained undefined. Over the next fifteen years, illegal drug traffic was treated as a minor item on the bilateral agenda and was tightly controlled within the established structure of permanent cooperation. Then, in 1985, the tragic murder of a U.S. Drug Enforcement Administration agent in Mexico unleashed a complex, new cycle of conflict that once again positioned the drug problem as one of the most sensitive issues facing the United States and Mexico.

This historical pattern of sporadic attention to a matter of undeniable interest to both countries—the illegal drug trade—suggests that something is missing from the bilateral relationship. Efforts to deal directly with the subject, without mixing it up with other aspects of bilateral relations, have been hampered by the absence of a shared diagnosis of the problem and by the lack of firm, permanent bases for dialogue. The general pattern of bilateral discussion and handling of the problem has been unbalanced and asymmetrical; the diagnosis and prescriptions, as well as concrete policy measures, have for the most part come from the United States. Until very recently, such decisions have paid little heed to Mexico's interests and concerns.

Drug trafficking is an area of special concern for governments because of the crime, violence, corruption, social disorder, individual destruction, and international tension that it engenders. Its increasing bilateral importance in the 1980s results from circumstances that are unlikely to disappear in the near future, and that could well deteriorate in the absence of a conscious, effective effort to turn back current trends. Two key factors are at work: first, we have the complex dynamic of the expanding drug trade as an international phenomenon that goes beyond the limits of any one country or any single bilateral relationship; second, we have the overtly political context and content of national and bilateral discussions of the subject. The political debate on drug trafficking has been dominated by distorted interpretations of the problem and conceptually erroneous or incomplete prescriptions for its resolution, which in turn have laid the groundwork for the adoption of intransigent unilateral policies, mutual recriminations, and the indefinite continuation of an unbalanced and inefficient international system for combating the flow of illegal drugs.

A Growing Problem

The increasing magnitude of the international drug trade has posed a direct challenge to governmental authority. The world drug market has been expanding constantly since the 1960s, but in the late 1970s and early 1980s the rhythm of expansion picked up alarmingly. This is particularly significant for Western Hemisphere countries, which include the world's largest and most dynamic drug consumer market—the United States—as well as important heroin and marijuana production zones and the entire world cocaine output. Narcotics have penetrated virtually every sector of U. S. society, creating a market of approximately 25 million regular consumers and annual profits of more than $100 billion. Drugs provide U. S. organized crime with its principal source of income and drugs have come to be seen in the United States as a critical threat to public health, social order, and national and local security.

Production has increased as well. New regions outside the twelve countries that traditionally have been centers of drug production have joined the global network.[1] Cultivation and output in traditional zones have meanwhile continued to increase despite the explosion of supply from the Third World, where precarious economic conditions have made drug production a highly attractive activity.

While it is true that the destructive impact of the illicit drug trade is internationally recognized, it is important to understand that the nature of the problem in *consuming* countries, plagued by high rates of drug abuse and addiction, is fundamentally different from the nature of the problem in *producing* countries. Organized

---

[1]The twelve traditional producers: Afghanistan, Bolivia, Burma, Colombia, Ecuador, Iran, Laos, Lebanon, Mexico, Pakistan, Peru, Thailand. For a current survey of global production trends—with the important exception of the United States—see U.S. Department of State, Bureau of International Narcotics Matters, *International Narcotics Control Strategy Report, March 1989* (Washington,D.C.), pp. 19-24.

crime and associated corruption are shared problems at both ends of the chain, but the distinct outcomes arising from these common problems in different countries give rise to varied and contrasting visions of the best way to deal with the issue. In this context the high level of public interest severely inhibits communication, understanding, and policy coordination between countries that occupy different positions in the international drug market's production-consumption chain.

The Political Framework

The global drug trade is not merely an economic question of supply and demand. The myriad, disruptive effects of drug trafficking and associated activities have become so entrenched and widespread as to exert serious impact on internal and external economic, strategic, and political issues and policy questions.

The drug problem touches sensitive points throughout society. It threatens perceptions of political authority, in terms of territorial and political control, political legitimacy, rule of law, and the effectiveness of police and security forces. It threatens the very foundations of society by fomenting crises in its basic institutions, eroding cultural values, and disrupting the work ethic. It affects the international relations of countries where it has taken root. Consequently, the need to bring the drug trade under control is a concern for entire societies as well as for governments.

From the U.S. perspective, according to some experts, international treatments of the drug problem touch on questions of national security. For the United States, the drug question is inseparable from such issues as international terrorism, communist subversion, arms traffic, the potential for social and political instability in the Third World, military and economic foreign aid, and control of its borders in the face of ever-increasing immigration flows. Thus the U.S. interpretation of the hemispheric and global agenda directly and explicitly links the drug problem with other, seemingly independent, vital issues in its so-called global effort to revitalize its world hegemony. Concurrently, the drug problem is becoming more and more important in relation to sensitive internal political issues, which in turn results in increased public interest and pressure.

The anti-drug policies of the Reagan Administration took on the character of a moral crusade. It was not merely a question of maintaining the legitimacy and credibility of a Republican government, according to this perspective, but of returning to a state of internal social equilibrium and economic productivity that would set the stage for the United States to regain its predominant role in world affairs. The increased importance of the drug problem as part of America's national and foreign policy political agenda has had the effect of making diplomatic and bilateral treatment of the issue much more complex and difficult than in the past.

Mexico has attached much less political importance than the United States to the drug problem, even as it has given continuous and high priority to actual efforts to combat the production, commercialization, and consumption of narcotics. Yet the drug issue has simply not acquired in Mexico the national political stature that it has in the United States. This can be attributed to the relatively low level of national drug use, which means that the pernicious effects of drugs on society and the economy are of secondary importance. (There are, however, certain regions of Mexico where opium poppy and marijuana cultivation is a primary economic activity, and where the economic and political consequences of drug money and drug trafficking activity have penetrated virtually every stratum of regional life.) These differences in the relative impact of drug trafficking explain, in part, why the drug problem has become one of the most important items on the bilateral agenda at the insistence of the United States instead of Mexico.

As the drug problem all over the world has continued its exponential increase, Mexico has begun to pay more attention to the issues, channelling more resources toward drug control. This, along with continuing pressure from the United States, has created a greater awareness of the problem in the Mexican public. It has not, however, added a new political dimension to the issue in Mexico.

The Bilateral Framework

The increased importance that the United States has attached to the international drug problem has had a strong and negative effect on the political atmosphere of U.S.-Mexican relations. This is due not only to the fact that the fight against drugs touches on sensitive national security and political issues in both countries, but also because of the manner in which the United States has expressed its concern. The strengthening of anti-drug policies in the U. S., in part a reaction to internal pressures, is reflected in the intensification and multiplication of various forms of unilateral pressure directed in general at principal drug-producing countries—and in particular at Mexico.

The dominant belief in the United States has been that the root of the drug problem is in the availability of narcotics, not the existence of an extensive and growing demand for them. This has led the U. S. government to concentrate its fight against drugs outside the country, transferring the costs and responsibilities of the fight to governments in drug-producing zones. This unbalanced manner of dealing with the problem has been a source of conflict and tension, undermining the political atmosphere of bilateral relations. Furthermore, it appears that this external focus has been largely based on the costs and difficulties likely to be involved in carrying the battle against drugs into the area of consumption.[2]

The strength of the United States public consensus with regard to the drug problem, made possible in part through political and ideological machinations, further contributes to erosion of the bilateral relationship. Apparently, the subject of drugs is often used by political and bureaucratic groups as an instrument for influencing aspects of United States-Mexican relations that are not directly related to the drug issue. Domestically, political manipulation of the drug problem has been used to attract votes and to achieve a high level of national consensus on other foreign policy and internal political issues, such as immigration or the question of Central America. This is a subject, then, capable of exercising indirect but significant influence over other specific items on the regional agenda to such an extent that any increase in its political visibility serves only to increase conflict and complexity in the bilateral negotiation process.

GROUNDS FOR A NEW PERSPECTIVE

During the next few years, the need to curtail the bilateral drug trade and to reduce the level of conflict it engenders will pose an inescapable challenge to the conduct of United States-Mexican relations. Both countries should make it a fundamental goal to transform the issue from a constant source of tension to an area of effective cooperation in the fight against a shared evil. This can

---

[2]Some of these costs are attributable to the negative impact of reinforcing law enforcement, and to the violations of individual and civil rights that might follow.

only be achieved through bilateral dialogue and a critical, objective review of present strategies.

Toward this end, it is necessary to identify the harsh reality beneath the public rhetoric. The problems involved in obtaining credible data make this task a particularly difficult one because of the nature of the activity under study—activity that takes place outside of the law, in the service of hidden interests. In any event, any alternative point of view must be based on a balanced, global understanding of the issue. The drug problem is:

• A worldwide, transnational problem that overruns national borders and specific bilateral relationships and that has differing consequences in different countries, depending on their particular circumstances.

• A series of overlapping, illegal activities in which drug production, distribution, and consumption are all distinct facets of a single, overarching phenomenon.

• A problem with multiple causes and multiple effects, at both the national and international level. Its myriad political, social, cultural, economic, law enforcement, and legal aspects require a multidisciplinary approach to its resolution.

• A problem that brings enormous social, economic, political, and public security costs to affected countries, generated both by the activities specific to it and by the policies and actions intended to combat it.

The Global View

The drug problem presents Mexico and the United States with critical challenges at the national level, the bilateral level, and the international level. Because the problem exists simultaneously on these three levels, the adoption of policies to combat it on each plane must be based on a common, shared understanding of the nature of the entire phenomenon.[3]

---

[3]In this essay the word "drug" is a generic term that represents a large variety of illicit or controlled substances, used for non-medicinal purposes, which can cause negative health effects and psychological and behavioral changes in the user. Although we use the terms "drug" and "narcotic" interchangeably in reference to a wide range of natural and synthetic, illegal and/or controlled substances, these terms have distinct connotations in keeping with classifications of substances

The formulation of an accurate diagnosis of the magnitude and character of the drug trade as it pertains to U. S.-Mexican relations requires appreciation of the wider context of the transnational world drug market. This global outlook is vital to an understanding of the factors that contribute to the continuing expansion of the bilateral drug trade in the face of efforts to control it. Furthermore, it is necessary to take such a global view in order to comprehend the limits inherent in any bilateral strategy for the containment of drug trafficking.

It is absolutely essential to understand that demand and supply are mutually dependent facets of a single problem. Producers and users of narcotics are linked together by a series of illegal and highly lucrative steps, from one end of the drug chain to the other. Drug use and drug traffic are two sides of the same coin which must be attacked simultaneously, with full awareness of their linkage, in any effective effort to combat the problem.

In the past, as Samuel del Villar shows in his essay in this volume, efforts to define and understand the drug problem have been excessively narrow. They have separated the *demand* for drugs, made up of dependence, addiction, and improper drug use in general[4] from the problems created by the conglomeration of illegal activities linked to the *supply* side of the equation, such as drug production, processing, transport, and commercialization. Such an

---

according to their particular characteristics. The World Health Organization (WHO) has developed eight classes of drugs, distinguished by their effects and the general behavior patterns associated with their use: 1) the alcohol-barbituates group (depressants); 2) amphetamines and stimulants; 3) cannabis, which produces strong sensations and pleasurable feelings; 4) cocaine, a stimulant which causes a sensation of euphoria; 5) hallucinogens, which cause perceptual distortion; 6) opiates (natural and synthetic substances which relieve pain and produce a state of lethargy); 7) volatile solvents (intoxicants and hallucinogens); and 8) tobacco (a stimulant). In general, this study basically focuses on marijuana, heroin, and cocaine because of their importance in the illegal drug trade between Mexico and the United States. We include the issue of synthetic, "dangerous" drugs as a secondary consideration.

[4]There are many patterns of improper drug use that can be defined as illicit, since improper drug use includes any non-medical use of mind-altering substances. In general, the line between accepted and improper drug use is drawn in accordance with international law as a legal point which limits acceptable drug use to that which has a medically justifiable purpose. There are numerous problems inherent in establishing the lines of separation between improper but moderate drug use, excessive drug abuse, and drug addiction or dependency—problems that arise from differing technical, scientific, and medical criteria for defining levels of addiction and dependency. In the absence of concrete definitions, principal statistics on drug consumption and international efforts to control drug trafficking have defined improper or unlawful drug use as that which has no medical purpose.

incomplete vision of the phenomenon bears the risk that government strategies for combatting it will also be incomplete, incoherent, inefficient, and inadequate.

The uncoordinated and unbalanced policy approaches evident throughout this century offer clear evidence of the traditional, disparate treatment of the issue. For the past fifty years, a conceptual gap has separated those who emphasize the importance of controlling the drug supply from those who consider it more important to reduce demand. Both points of view have a certain degree of validity, but the time has come to close—or at least to lessen—the gap that keeps them apart.

A global understanding of the drug phenomenon is necessary to formulate general guidelines for new approaches to the problem, founded on negotiation and international cooperation. The drug trade is not merely the responsibility of those who are directly linked to illegal drug cultivation, processing, transport, and distribution. All those individuals who buy small quantities of drugs for their personal use share responsibility for the problem too, because they constitute the economic base that allows drug traffickers to finance the whole chain of illegitimate activities involved in bringing drugs to consumers. As long as efforts to choke off the drug supply at its source are unaccompanied by simultaneous efforts to attack the factors contributing to drug demand there will always be an overriding economic incentive to keep producing drugs somewhere in the world, and to transport and distribute those drugs to the consumers.

As the Bilateral Commission asserts in its report,[5] drug consuming countries and drug producing countries should therefore share responsibility in dealing with the problem. It is the collective responsibility of the entire international community to make a coordinated, consistent, permanent, and simultaneous attack on each and every link in the drug market chain.

Strategies for confronting specific aspects of the problem should be designed with the understanding that the international drug market is not a perfectly balanced monolith. There are asymmetries among the different aspects of the drug trade, and policy efforts should be balanced in proportion to the resources,

---

[5]*The Challenge of Interdependence: Mexico and the United States* (Lanham, Md.: University Press of America, 1988), ch. 4.

importance, and market position of each country. The distribution
of effort should be based on an objective evaluation of the work-
ings of the world narcotics market. Countries which play different roles, with different degrees of importance, in the world drug
market suffer quantitatively and qualitatively different social,
economic, political, and cultural consequences from their participation in it. A global view of the drug phenomenon as a whole
allows us to recognize areas of convergence and divergence
between countries which, while sharing interest in—and responsibility for—the common problem, are affected by it in diverse and
unequal ways.

Drug traffic between the United States and Mexico can thus
be understood within the context of a global market that exhibits
several defining characteristics.[6] One central feature of this market is the high degree of *interdependence* between its component
parts. Drug transportation and distribution networks tend to be
based in distinct geographic zones and groups of countries, as are
production and consumption centers. This leads to the establish-
ment of strong relationships based on mutual dependence between
countries in different positions along the production- consumption
chain, but it does not reduce the levels of inequality in the importance of those countries' relative positions in the market. While the
world drug supply comes from a relatively large number of producing countries (some twelve to twenty countries are consistent
drug producers, though their relative importance with regard to
the total world drug supply may fluctuate widely),[7] a single country on the side of demand—the United States—accounts for the
largest and most dynamic drug market in the world. Its position
as the world's largest, most concentrated retail narcotics market

---

[6]The considerations that follow are quite general, but they appear to be common to
the phenomenon in all its aspects throughout the world. Nonetheless, it is important to stress that each type of drug represents distinct problems and circumstances
due to differing production conditions, supply situations, and consumption patterns.
On both the demand and supply sides, geographic distribution and concentration
of the market, along with distribution networks' organization levels, vary depending on the specific drug in question.

[7]The criteria we use to identify drug-producing countries are: an annual production level (in cultivation and/or processing) of at least five metric tons of opium,
500 metric tons of coca leaf, and 500 metric tons of marijuana; and the existence of
drug eradication programs as reported in information collected by the National
Narcotics Intelligence Consumers Committee (an agency dedicated to coordinating official U.S. government estimates on drug matters). Not only is there a relatively large and diverse group of drug producing countries, but the number of
potential alternative producers is also quite high.

augments its importance as a determinant of the drug trade's global dynamic.[8]

Over the past decade, there has been an increase in countries that have active markets in both drug production and consumption. There has been a tendency for drug production to rise in countries with strong internal indices of consumption on the one hand, and for increased drug use in producing zones on the other. This has contributed to a significant, albeit gradual, transformation of the bases of international political and academic debate on the issue over the past fifty years, clearing the way for increasing acceptance of a comprehensive understanding of the problem in drug consuming countries as well as producing ones. This new perception emphasizes the dual nature of the drug problem, the mutually dependent relationship between supply and demand as two sides of the same question, and it constitutes an important first step towards reformulation of international policies for dealing with the issue.

Second, the commercialization of illicit drugs has come to generate enormous *profitability*. But one of the characteristics of the drug trade, which in itself serves to reinforce patterns of disproportionate interdependence, is that different links in the chain do not share equally in these profits. The costs associated with the initial stages of drug commercialization in producing countries— cultivation, processing, and transportation to exit ports—account for only some 8 percent of the final value of drugs in retail markets.[9]

---

[8]The importance of the United States as the principal drug consumption market in the world, as measured by the number of consumers, quantity of drugs consumed, and economic weight of the market, varies depending on different sources of supply and with regard to different kinds of drugs. For example, the market for heroin and opium in the United States is an important, but not dominant, factor in the expansion of output of those substances in their principal production zones. Estimates indicate that the European heroin market is similar in proportion to that of the U.S. (between six and seven metric tons per year), and that sources of production in Southwest Asia also account for an important percentage of heroin consumption, with some 1.2 million heroin addicts and 2 million opium users concentrated in India, Pakistan, Iran, and Afghanistan. The cocaine market, on the other hand, is much more highly concentrated: between 105 and 107 metric tons of cocaine were imported into the United States in 1985, while less than 20 metric tons reached the European market; local consumption in cocaine production zones has grown in recent years, but it is a significant problem only in Colombia. The United States is also the principal world retail market for marijuana, accounting for consumption of between 7,500 and 11,650 metric tons of the drug in 1986.
[9]These estimates are derived from NNICC data, elaborated by Peter Reuter in *Eternal Hope: America's International Narcotics Efforts*, (Washington, D.C.: The Rand Corporation, Mimeograph), February 1983.

Economic estimates tend to be unreliable, due to the illegality of drug activity, but data on prices along the commercialization process suggest that the most profitable activities take place at the retail end of the chain.[10] For every dollar spent on marijuana in the U.S., marijuana-growing peasants earn between seven and nine cents; cocaine producers earn one to three cents out of every dollar spent by users to support their habit and; only seven or eight cents of every dollar spent on heroin goes to producers of the drug.[11]

Third, the world drug market has over the last twenty-five years developed a fluid and dynamic *adaptability* that gives rise to ever-new social and public health ills. Significant but short-term fluctuations in production levels in the relative contributions of different supply sources are absorbed without noticeable effect at the retail level, as illicit drug networks develop new production and refining methods as well as new transportation routes. This ability to adapt and innovate is attributable in part to the immense resources commanded by drug traffickers, which allow them to rapidly and effectively adjust to any reinforcement of anti-drug policies. Even as efforts to combat it have grown stronger, the illegal drug market has over the years responded to substantial changes in both supply and demand while continuing its pattern of constant growth fueled by lavish profits.

Fourth, the *illegality* of the drug trade and the *uneven penalties* meted out to lawbreakers—on the side of demand or supply—are significant factors in the market's economic operation. The level of risk involved at every stage of the illegal market keeps drug prices well above the real costs of drug production.[12] In fact, some experts suggest that the very characteristics of the longstanding international system for controlling and prosecuting participation

---

[10]W. Lee Rensselaer, "The Drug Trade and Developing Countries," *Policy Focus*, 4, May 1987 (Washington, D.C.: Overseas Development Council), details the differences in drug prices at the wholesale and retail levels. From wholesale prices at the source to retail prices in the United States: marijuana goes from $770-$1,540 to $1,550-$3,450 per kilo; cocaine goes from $30,000-$50,000 to $600,000-$650,000 per kilo; a kilo of heroin is worth $95,000-$197,000 per wholesale kilo, rising to $1,550,000-$1,650,000 per kilo on the retail market.

[11]See Peter Reuter and Mark A. R. Kleiman, "Risks and Prices: an Economic Analysis of Drug Enforcement," in Michael Tonry and Norval Morris, eds., *Crime and Justice: An Annual Review of Research*, 7 (July 1986): 293.

[12]The economic consequences of drugs' illegality are fully analyzed in Mark A. Moore, "Drug Policy and Organized Crime," prepared for the report of the President's Commission on Organized Crime, *Report to the President and Attorney General. America's Habit: Drug Abuse, Drug Trafficking and Organized Crime* (Washington, D.C.: U.S. Government Printing Office, 1986).

in the narcotics market are important factors in the growth of the market itself.[13] Current approaches to the problem, treating drug use with relative tolerance while energetically attacking drug production, contribute to high drug prices which in turn provide the prime motivation for the expansion of drug supply.

This general overview serves as the foundation for a diagnosis of current tendencies in illegal drug traffic between Mexico and the United States. One must also consider the relative importance of both countries in the world market, in terms of drug production and consumption. And it is important to assess both the causes of the problem and the policies employed in each country as they relate to patterns and levels of drug production, traffic, and consumption.

General trends in the bilateral drug trade during the 1980s suggest that the steadily growing drug trade will continue to be a serious problem in coming years in spite of stepped-up efforts to control it. It has expanded on every front, on both sides of the U.S.-Mexican border, in both quantitative terms (levels of demand, supply, and economic worth) and qualitative terms (widening and deepening of the negative effects of drug production and consumption on social, cultural, economic, and political structures). The matter has grown so serious that it will remain an important issue for the foreseeable future—in spite of an encouraging trend towards decreasing consumption levels in the United States, the intensification of efforts to reduce Mexican heroin and marijuana production, and the acceleration of measures to dismantle the Mexican cocaine pipeline.

During the next few decades the United States and Mexico will be faced with the challenge of reversing, on both sides of the border, the expansionist tendencies inherent in the drug commercialization process. To do so effectively they will need to take simultaneous actions against both supply and demand, and they will have to coordinate their actions at all levels. While the problem is common to both countries, the great disparities between their positions in regard to drug consumption, production and traffic,

---

[13]Galen Carpenter, *The U.S. Campaign Against International Narcotics Trafficking: A Cure Worse Than the Disease*, Cato Institute (Mimeograph), December, 1985; Peter Reuter, *Eternal Hope* and Samuel I. del Villar, "La narcotización de la cultura en Estados Unidos y su impacto en México," in Gabriel Székely, ed., *México-Estados Unidos 1985* (México, D.F.: El Colegio de México, 1986).

mean that it manifests itself differently and unevenly in each country. It is vitally important for Mexico and the United States to understand their different roles in the market in order to wage a coordinated, effective battle against narcotics.

IN THIS VOLUME

The Bilateral Commission on the Future of U.S.-Mexican Relations has emphasized the drug problem as one of its major areas of concern and devoted an entire chapter of its report to this subject. This reflects not only the increasing importance of drugs on the bilateral agenda, and as a domestic concern in both countries, but also the evolution of the drug problem within an arena of negotiation and conflict where the challenges of increasing interdependence between Mexico and the United States are particularly well defined.

The Commission's discussions of the drug problem were shaped by the paradoxical contradiction between the obvious convergence of the national interests of both countries in combatting drugs and the enormous difficulty of establishing a smooth, stable framework for bilateral cooperation for doing so. A second factor that contributed to the Commission's approach was the clear necessity for attempting to distinguish between rhetoric and reality in academic and political debates. The issue is highly visible to the public, but because of its illegal, transnational nature its actual dimensions are little-known and under-studied.

With these considerations in mind a workshop on drug traffic was held in Querétaro in August 1987, with the participation of academic experts as well as policy actors responsible for the formulation and implementation of antidrug policies in both countries. The goal of the workshop was to generate open, pluralistic, and objective discussion based on systematic research and study, in order to facilitate an integrated view of the problem and realistic determination of its size.

This volume presents some of the results of these efforts. Studies from the Querétaro conference—highly academic works that offered new ideas for defining and refining policy debates—have been culled for this book in order to focus discussion on two key issues: the realities of the international drug market and policy options. Not all papers from the workshop are included here, but this introductory essay emerges from the workshop as a whole and thus owes many of its ideas to studies that are absent from this volume.

This book covers a wide range of opinions and viewpoints expressed by both Americans and Mexicans. They deal with different aspects of the phenomenon and, as a result, the policy recommendations developed from them lead in different directions and do not necessarily converge.

The first part of the book is concerned with the two key elements of the illegal drug market in the context of U.S.-Mexican relations: U.S. demand and Mexican supply. Ann Blanken's paper describes some current elements and possible future tendencies of drug consumption in U.S. society and defines the problem of illegal drug use throughout wide sectors of society as an issue that affects practically every level of social, political, economic, police, and diplomatic conduct in the country. Recent survey data lead Blanken to suggest that there is a relative lessening in the general tendency towards drug consumption, but that the United States will still continue to constitute the biggest, most dynamic, strongest demand market for drugs in the world.

Miguel Ruiz-Cabañas's study is concerned with the ever-changing role of the supply of drugs produced or brought into the market in Mexico for U.S. consumption. The historical perspective of this essay leads to two central conclusions: first, that Mexico's geography and socioeconomic and environmental conditions have led to its being a consistent source for the supply of marijuana and heroin in the United States throughout this century; second, that the relative importance Mexico as a source of illegal drugs has undergone significant fluctuations and changes over time, due to Mexican antidrug policies as well as to variations in levels of drug production in other parts of the world. Given the characteristics of a transnational world drug market backed by enormous economic resources, Ruiz-Cabañas suggests that policies for combatting drugs will be ineffective over the long run unless they overcome national and bilateral limits and adopt an international strategy that puts equal emphasis on the problems of supply and demand.

The second part of the book deals with the antidrug policies that have been implemented in Mexico and the United States since the early part of this century. Richard Craig argues that the United

States has had a clear and consistent drug policy, international in scope but inefficient in practice. Some of this international policy's inherent contradictions have been especially manifest in the context of U.S.-Mexican relations. Craig highlights the excessive emphasis on restricting supply, the unilateral adoption of policy prescriptions, the demagogic manipulation of antidrug policy, and the tendency to create incidents as some of the characteristics of U.S. diplomacy towards Mexico with respect to the drug problem that have negatively affected bilateral cooperation not only in the fight against drugs but along the whole gamut of issues. At the end of his paper, Craig makes some suggestions for adjusting U.S. international antidrug policy without making any radical changes in its fundamental premises—something that would be practically impossible in light of present political conditions in the United States—thus reducing the potential for political-diplomatic tensions.

Samuel I. del Villar's contribution is a cost-benefit analysis, from the Mexican point of view and in the context of the segments of the drug market that pertain to Mexico, of the Mexican government's official antidrug policies. Del Villar argues that the principal cause of all the problems associated with drug cultivation, production, and traffic in Mexico lies beyond Mexico's borders. It is, in fact, the existence of a large and dynamic demand for drugs in the United States. This explains why Mexico's strict laws and punishments directed against the drug market and the permanent campaigns established in 1968 to destroy crops, intercept drug-carrying vehicles, and prosecute drug traffickers have had little effect even as their costs have been enormously high. Del Villar uses this analysis to support a call for a new interpretation of the drug problem and, similarly, a redefinition of current policies in Mexico as well as in the United States.

The appendices to this volume are designed to supply basic but not readily available information for general reference and for use in future studies of Mexico's role in the world drug market. They include two documents prepared by Miguel Ruiz-Cabañas with data from the United Nations, in which he describes some recent trends in the international supply of illegal drugs in light of official figures on drug seizures worldwide and the percentage of those seizures made by Mexico.

SECTION

I

THE TWO FACES
OF THE PROBLEM

2

Changing Patterns of Drug Abuse in the United States

Ann J. Blanken

Drug abuse is a major social problem in the United States today. Public concern about drug abuse is reflected in the formation of parent groups in our communities and "Just Say No" clubs in our schools, in state laws prohibiting the sale of drug paraphernalia, in national legislation providing direction and resources to address the drug abuse problem on various fronts, and in continuing media coverage. The degree of attention and activity focused on drug abuse might be interpreted to mean that drug abuse is a new problem; this, of course, is not the case.

This paper provides an overview of drug abuse patterns and trends in the United States. Following a brief historical review, the essay presents data on recent trends in the prevalence of illicit drug use as well as data on demographic and geographic variations in use patterns. Trends in adverse health consequences associated with drug abuse as reflected in emergency room, medical examiner, and treatment data are described in the third section, followed by a discussion of a number of the factors—e.g., the use of multiple drugs and available street drugs—which contribute to the complex and dynamic nature of observed drug abuse patterns. The final section underscores the need for a continuing, long-term commitment to address issues associated with drug abuse. Brief descriptions of national data systems are provided as an appendix.

The views expressed in this paper are those of the author and are not meant to represent the official position of the National Institute on Drug Abuse or the Department of Health and Human Services.

HISTORICAL OVERVIEW

An ancient problem for mankind, addiction to psychoactive drugs developed as a problem in the United States in the middle of the nineteenth century. Important events in the evolution of drug use at that time were the importation of Chinese laborers, the perfection of the hypodermic syringe, and the Civil War. In addition, opium- and cocaine-containing products were widely available from physicians and from drug and grocery stores.[1] Most of the estimated 250,000 addicts in the United States were women.[2] There were few regulations and, continuing into the early twentieth century, no laws requiring the labeling of the ingredients of these preparations.

The turn of the century brought changes—both in public attitudes and legislation. The Pure Food and Drug Act of 1906 required that manufacturers list ingredients on their labels. The Harrison Narcotic Act of 1914, which was originally intended as a revenue measure, required that anyone producing or distributing opiates or cocaine register with the federal government and keep records of all transactions. Through legal interpretation, this law eventually prohibited supplying narcotics to addicts, even with a physician's prescription.[3] By 1924, the manufacture and importation of heroin was prohibited in the United States. Most importation of cocaine and coca leaves was prohibited by an amendment in 1922 to the Narcotic Drugs Import and Export Act. Thus, the use of heroin and cocaine was forced underground.

Just as a number of factors had coalesced a century earlier to spur addiction in the United States, events of the 1960s brought another round of changes in the composition and dimension of the drug abuse problem. Drug use was to play a central role as American youth rejected middle-class values and marijuana use became a symbol for the counterculture. As the revolution in drug use continued well into the 1970s, it appeared that at least experimenting with illicit drugs became a rite of passage for the nation's youth. It also became apparent that scientific data were needed to describe and assess the new trends.[4] During the early 1970s, several national

[1]O.S. Ray, *Drugs, Society and Human Behavior* (St. Louis: C.V. Moshy Company, 1974).
[2]W. Cuskey, T. Premkumar, and L. Sigel, "Survey of Opiate Addiction among Females in the United States between 1850 and 1970," *Psychotherapy and Drug Addiction* 1 (1974).
[3]E.M. Brecher, *The Editors of Consumer Reports: Licit and Illicit Drugs* (Boston-Toronto: Little, Brown and Co., 1972).
[4]The application of epidemiologic approaches to the study of drug abuse began less than two decades ago. The use of the term "epidemic" to describe drug abuse came

data collection systems were designed and implemented to quantify and describe the national drug abuse problem. Two of these systems—the National Household Survey on Drug Abuse and the High School Senior Survey—are cross-sectional surveys which directly measure the prevalence of drug abuse. Two other systems were designed to measure particular subsets of drug abusers: those requiring treatment for drug abuse, collected through the Client Oriented Data Acquisition Process (CODAP); those experiencing drug abuse-related medical emergencies, collected through the Drug Abuse Warning Network (DAWN); and those who died, also collected through DAWN. Key attributes of each of these systems are described in the appendix. Their importance resides in the information they furnish about the prevalence and health-related consequences of drug use in the United States.

NATURE AND EXTENT OF DRUG ABUSE IN THE UNITED STATES

This section presents data which describe the overall prevalence of and recent trends in drug abuse in the United States. As documented by the available data, prevalence levels vary according to type of drug used, demographic characteristics, and region of the country.

According to the National Household Survey on Drug Abuse, more than one-third of all Americans over the age of 11 have used a drug illicitly at least once in their lives. Illicit drug use includes nonmedical use of psychotherapeutic drugs as well as use of heroin, cocaine, marijuana, inhalants, or hallucinogens. Among young adults 18-25 years of age, the subgroup with the highest rates of drug abuse, the proportion is closer to two-thirds. By far, marijuana is the most commonly used illicit drug. Nearly one in ten Americans, or eighteen million, were current users of marijuana in 1985. Current use is defined as used at least once in the thirty days prior to being interviewed in the National Household Survey on Drug Abuse. By way of comparison, nearly six in ten were current users of the legal drug alcohol, and three in ten were current users of

---

into vogue during the outbreak of heroin abuse in the late 1960s. Issues such as the "voluntary" nature of drug use in contrast to involuntarily contracted diseases were considered as scientific debate centered on the appropriateness of using epidemiologic tools in addressing the drug abuse problem. Through such debate, however, it became clear that epidemiologic approaches were appropriate and the introduction of epidemiology to the study of drug abuse was not seriously impeded (N.J. Kozen and E. H. Adams, "Epidemiology of Drug Abuse: An Overview," *Science* 234 [1986]).

cigarettes. As shown in table 1, cocaine is the most frequently reported illicit drug following marijuana.

Table 1. Prevalence of Use of Selected Drugs among Persons 12 Years and Older: United States, 1985

	Ever Used		Used in Past Month	
	%	Population Estimate (millions)	%	Population Estimate (millions)
Marijuana	33	61.9	10	18.2
Hallucinogens	7	12.8	0.5	.96
Inhalants	7	12.9	1	1.9
Cocaine	12	22.2	3	5.8
Nonmedical Use:				
Stimulants	9	17.6	1	2.7
Sedatives	6	11.5	1	1.7
Tranquilizers	8	14.8	1	2.2
Analgesics	7	12.6	1	2.5
Alcohol	86	164.4	59	113.1
Cigarettes	76	144.5	32	60.3

Source: National Institute on Drug Abuse, 1985 National Household Survey on Drug Abuse.

Drug use estimates derived from the national prevalence surveys must be viewed as conservative in general since some of the nonsampled populations, such as persons with no fixed address and prisoners, have higher rates of drug abuse than does the general population.[5] Additionally, sample surveys are not sensitive enough to measure rare events reliably. These considerations are pertinent to explaining why heroin use is not presented in table 1. Since heroin use is both a relatively rare event and disproportionately represented in nonsampled populations, various attempts have been made over the years to estimate heroin prevalence using techniques such as mathematical modeling of indirect indicator data.[6] One such estimate indicated that there were approximately half a million heroin addicts/users in the United States in 1981.[7]

[5]C.B. Kalish and W.T. Masumura, *Prisoners and Drugs, Bureau of Justice Statistics Bulletin*, DOJ Document (NCJ) 87-575 (Washington, D.C.: U.S. Government Printing Office, March 1983); New York State Division of Substance Abuse Services, "Drug Use among Tenants of Single Room Occupancy (S.R.O.) Hotels in New York City," unpublished paper, New York City, 1983.

[6]M.D. Brodsky, "History of Heroin Prevalence Estimation Techniques," in *Self-Report Methods of Estimating Drug Use: Meeting Current Challenges to Validity*, ed. B.A. Rouse, N.J. Kozel, and L.G. Richards. NIDA Research Monograph no. 57, DHHS Publication (ADM)85-1402 (Washington, D.C.: U.S. Government Printing Office, 1985).

[7]National Narcotics Intelligence Consumers Committee, *The NNICC Report 1985-1986* (Washington, D.C.: NNICC, 1987).

The adequacy of such estimates is difficult to assess since they are not based on classical statistical techniques. Research continues on the development of alternative estimation techniques, including the application of methodologies developed in other fields, e.g., mental health.

The data in table 1 clearly indicate that a large segment of the American population has had some experience, at least to the extent of experimentation, with illicit drugs. By the 1980s, Americans, particularly young Americans, had lost their innocence regarding illicit drug use—a major departure from the norm two decades earlier. While no national epidemiologic studies of drug abuse were conducted in the early 1960s, some indication of the enormous magnitude of the increase in illicit drug use during the 1960s and 1970s is provided by retrospective data collected by the 1977 National Survey on Drug Abuse. For successive cohorts of young adults aged 18-25, it is estimated that: in 1962, only 4 percent had ever tried marijuana; in 1967, 13 percent had done so; and by 1979, 68 percent had at least tried marijuana.[8] Marijuana use was no longer restricted to the counterculture.

It now appears that the ever-increasing spread of drug abuse reached its zenith in the late 1970s. Since the 1979 peak of 68 percent, the proportion of 18-25 year-olds who had ever tried marijuana decreased to 64 percent in 1982 and to 61 percent in 1985. A similar pattern has been observed for high school seniors. In 1975, the first year in which the survey was conducted, 47 percent of the high school senior class had ever tried marijuana. By 1979, this proportion had increased to 60 percent; yet throughout the 1980s, marijuana use gradually declined, reaching 51 percent of the class of 1986. An alternative measure—illicit drug use of any kind—revealed that approximately two-thirds of the students in each of the high school senior classes for the period 1979 to 1982 had tried marijuana and/or some other illicit drug. By 1986, the overall index of illicit drug use of any kind had declined to 58 percent.

One of the most striking and encouraging indicators of the apparent overall moderation in drug use levels in the United States is the trend in the estimated percent of high school seniors who use marijuana on a daily or near daily basis. In 1978, nearly one senior in nine used marijuana almost daily. By 1986, this statistic

---

[8] J.D. Miller and I.H. Cisin, *Highlights from the National Survey on Drug Abuse: 1979*, DHHS Publication (ADM)80-1032 (Washington, D.C.: U.S. Government Printing Office, 1980).

had dropped to one in twenty-five. In short, both indicators show declining propensity to use drugs among successive cohorts.

These optimistic scenarios must be tempered by noting that, despite declines in the overall levels of drug use, drug use remains at higher levels in the United States than in any other industrial nation. While perhaps encouraging from a long-term perspective, statistics showing that more than half of the nation's high school seniors have tried illicit drugs suggest that drug use is a serious social problem among American youth; these statistics cannot be dismissed lightly.

Not surprisingly, there are exceptions in the overall pattern of declining drug use according to factors such as drug type and population subgroup. Two notable exceptions are trends in cocaine use and trends for persons over 25 years of age. These patterns are illustrated in table 2.

Current marijuana use, which peaked among youth and young adults in the late 1970s, has remained at peak levels among persons over the age of 25 since 1979. Somewhat analogously, the level of current cocaine use by persons over 25, which was too low to measure reliably prior to 1979, reached 2.0 percent in 1985.

While current cocaine use peaked among 18-25 year-olds in 1979, no trend has developed since then, unlike the steady decline in marijuana use. Except for the peak of nearly 7 percent in 1985, the proportion of high school seniors currently using cocaine ranged roughly between 5 and 6 percent over the entire period from 1979 to 1986, again in contrast to the declining pattern for marijuana. A significant decline in current cocaine use was found, however, for the high school senior class of 1987. Use of hallucinogens, such as PCP and LSD, appears to be relatively uncommon and declining somewhat during the 1980s.

It has been estimated that the reduction in marijuana use between 1982 and 1985 resulted in a 4 percent reduction in consumption—from 4,889.8 metric tons to 4,693.9 metric tons. Cocaine consumption, on the other hand, increased substantially—from 31.0 metric tons of cocaine HCL in 1982 to 72.3 metric tons in 1985. At the retail, or "street," level, it was estimated that purities for gram quantities ranged from 50 to 60 percent during 1985 and 55 to 65 percent during 1986.[9]

---

[9]National Narcotics Intelligence Consumers Committee, *The NNICC Report 1985-1986*.

Table 2. Trends in Past Month Use of Selected Drugs: United States, 1974-1986

	1974	1977	1979	1982	1985		
Household Population:							
Age 12-17							
Marijuana	12.0%	16.6%	16.7%	11.5%[a]	12.0%		
Cocaine	1.0	0.8	1.4	1.6	1.5		
Hallucinogens	1.3	1.6	2.2	1.4	1.2		
Age 18-25							
Marijuana	25.2	27.4	35.4	27.4[a]	21.8[b]		
Cocaine	3.1	3.7	9.3	6.8[c]	7.6		
Hallucinogens	2.5	2.0	4.4	1.7[a]	1.9		
Age 26 and Older							
Marijuana	2.0	3.3	6.0[d]	6.5	6.1		
Cocaine	+	+	0.9	1.2	2.0		
Hallucinogens	+	+	+	+	+		

	1975	1977	1979	1982	1985	1986	1987
High School:							
Senior							
Marijuana	27.1	35.4	36.5	28.5	25.7	23.4	21.0[e]
Cocaine	1.9	2.9	5.7	5.0	6.7	6.2	4.3[e]
Hallucinogens	NA	NA	5.3	4.1	3.8	3.5	2.8
Any illicit drug use	30.7	37.6	38.9	32.5	29.7	27.1	24.7[e]

NA=Not available.
+Less than one-half of 1 percent.
[a]Difference between 1979 and 1982 statistically significant at the .001 level.
[b]Difference between 1982 and 1985 statistically significant at .01 level.
[c]Difference between 1979 and 1982 statistically significant at the .05 level.
[d]Difference between 1977 and 1979 statistically significant at the .001 level.
[e]Difference between 1986 and 1987 statistically significant at .001 level for cocaine, at .01 level for any illicit drug use, and at .05 level for marijuana.

Source: National Institute on Drug Abuse, National Household Survey on Drug Abuse and High School Senior Survey.

Overall, whites and blacks are more likely than are Hispanic Americans to use illicit drugs. For example, estimates for the 1985 National Household Survey show that while approximately one-third each of blacks and whites had ever tried marijuana, only about one-fourth of Hispanics had done so.[10] It should be noted, however, that other studies have shown that rates of drug use among Hispanics vary according to degree of acculturation as well as country of national origin. Data from the Hispanic Health and

---

[10]National Institute on Drug Abuse, *National Household Survey on Drug Abuse: Population Estimates, 1985*, DHHS Publication (ADM)87-1539 (Washington, D.C.: U.S. Government Printing Office, 1987).

Nutrition Examination Survey for persons 12 to 44 years of age show, for example, that persons of Puerto Rican origin residing in the New York City area were more likely to have used cocaine (22 percent) than were Mexican Americans residing in the southwestern United States (11 percent). Among Mexican Americans, those born in the United States were more likely to have used cocaine (14 percent) than were those born in Mexico (6 percent).[11]

Males are about one-third more likely than are females (42 percent compared to 32 percent) to have ever used an illicit drug and about two-thirds more likely to be a current user (15 percent versus 9 percent).[12] Similar overall relationships occur in each race/ethnic group.

When the data are controlled for age, sex, and race/ethnicity, two patterns of particular note and concern appear. One is that the male/female differentials are less pronounced among 12-17 year-olds than they are among older persons, particularly for whites. Among white youth, current use of any illicit drug, for example, was estimated to be 17 percent for males and 15 percent for females. Corresponding percentages for Hispanic youth are 14 percent for males and 11 percent for females. A larger sex differential was observed for black youth—13 percent for males compared to 8 percent for females.

The other particularly notable pattern pertains to black/white differentials. While rates for blacks tend to be lower than or similar to those for whites at younger ages, among males 35 and older, blacks are more likely than are whites to use illicit drugs. For example, an estimated 13 percent of black males aged 35 and older are current users of an illicit drug. In contrast, only 4 percent of white males of the same ages are current illicit drug users.

Drug abuse is often perceived as a big city or urban problem. While certain aspects of the drug abuse problem may be peculiar to big cities, the use of illicit substances is widespread in small towns as well as in major urban areas. The High School Senior Survey data presented in table 3 illustrate the geographic dispersion of drug abuse in that age group. While the level of current marijuana use in 1986 was highest among high school seniors in

---

[11]National Institute on Drug Abuse, *Use of Selected Drugs among Hispanics: Mexican-Americans, Puerto Ricans, Cuban-Americans*, DHHS Publication (ADM)87-1527 (Washington, D.C.: U.S. Government Printing Office, 1987).
[12]National Institute on Drug Abuse, *National Household Survey on Drug Abuse.*

Table 3. Past Month Use of Selected Drugs according to Population Density and Region: United States High School Seniors, 1986

	Marijuana	Cocaine	LSD	Stimulants (nonmedical use)
Population Density:				
Large SMSA*	26.7%	9.5%	1.5%	5.0%
Other SMSA*	22.9	5.6	1.8	5.6
Non-SMSA*	21.5	4.3	1.6	5.8
Region:				
Northeast	28.5	8.6	1.9	5.9
North Central	24.0	4.6	1.8	6.2
South	19.2	3.4	1.2	4.4
West	23.1	10.5	2.1	5.8

*SMSA is the acronym for Standard Metropolitan Statistical Area.

Source: National Institute on Drug Abuse, 1986 High School Senior Survey.

large metropolitan areas (27 percent), it was still substantial, involving more than one in five, among seniors living in less densely populated areas. The biggest relative differential occurred in the prevalence of current cocaine use, with seniors in large areas being more than twice as likely as were seniors living outside of Standard Metropolitan Statistical Areas (SMSAs) to be current cocaine users. In a somewhat similar fashion, almost one in five of the high school seniors residing in the area of the country with the lowest prevalence levels—the South—was a current marijuana user. Also, the largest regional differentials were for cocaine.

Most of the marijuana and cocaine consumed in the United States is consumed by a relatively small proportion of all users, those who are frequent users. Data from the 1985 National Household Survey indicate that approximately half of all persons who ever used marijuana and two-thirds of those who ever used cocaine did so ten times or less. Among those who used marijuana in the month prior to interview, nearly half did so on four days or less; 30 percent used marijuana on between five and nineteen days, and 22 percent used marijuana on twenty to thirty days. Data developed by clinical researchers indicate that frequent cocaine users consume a disproportionate amount of cocaine, not only because of the excess number of days on which the drug is used but also because frequent users use larger quantities per day than do less frequent users.[13]

[13]National Institute on Drug Abuse, "Methodology for Marijuana and Cocaine Consumption Estimates," unpublished documentation provided by J.C. Gfroerer, July 1987.

Overall prevalence trends describe the extent and spread of drug use in the general population; they do not measure, per se, problems associated with drug use. While problems and prevalence are inevitably linked, the relationship between them is not one to one. Thus, a decline in general prevalence levels does not necessarily mean that there will be an immediate, corresponding reduction in drug abuse-related problems or, for that matter, that the problems will not continue to escalate. The adverse consequences of drug abuse are manifested in many ways, including, but not limited to: poor performance at school or on the job; family problems; economic problems; health problems, including death; and crime. Since most of these consequences impact others in addition to the drug abusers themselves, the overall impact on society is far greater than the sum total of the individuals directly involved.

TRENDS IN ADVERSE HEALTH CONSEQUENCES

While this paper will not attempt to address the vast array of drug-related problems, the DAWN data described earlier are considered here as measures of specific adverse consequences, i.e., medical emergencies and death. Client treatment data also provide useful information on consequences, in this case, specifically for drug abusers who are suffering sufficient dysfunction in their lives to seek treatment. Since the DAWN data and the client treatment data are drawn from record sources which reflect those subsets of all drug abusers who are suffering particular adverse consequences, they do not measure prevalence of use per se.

Over the years, heroin has been the illicit drug mentioned most frequently in hospital emergency room visits and in medical examiner cases. Thus, although heroin use is relatively rare, it has been a major factor in the morbidity and mortality associated with drug abuse in the United States.

The number of heroin-related cases reported to DAWN has been increasing through the 1980s as shown in table 4. As indicated previously, changes in trends in consequences are not necessarily directly linked to prevalence trends; such would appear to be the case with the DAWN heroin trends. An analysis of the incidence of new heroin use based on treatment data indicated that the "preponderance of current heroin abusers were initiated into heroin abuse between the mid-1960s and mid-1970s."[14] Additionally,

---

[14]Kozel and Adams, "Epidemiology of Drug Abuse," p. 30.

DAWN data show that the average age of patients visiting an emergency room for a heroin-related problem increased from 26.8 years in 1976 to 32.1 years in 1985; similar increases were found in the medical examiner data.[15] Treatment client data also indicate that the average age of heroin clients has been increasing and that most clients admitted for the treatment of heroin abuse have had multiple treatment experiences.[16] Epidemiologic field investigations by staff of the National Institute on Drug Abuse have found that renewed or increased use by current or former heroin users are apparently the primary sources of increase noted in DAWN statistics. Thus, it would appear that the pool of heroin addicts has been relatively stable over the decade between the mid-1970s and mid-1980s; factors other than prevalence alone contributed to the increase in medical consequences reflected in table 4.

Table 4. Trends in Emergency Room (ER) and Medical Examiner (ME) Mentions of Heroin and Cocaine, and Emergency Room Mentions of Marijuana: United States, 1976-1985

	Heroin No. of Mentions		Cocaine No. of Mentions		Marijuana No. of Mentions
	ER	ME	ER	ME	ER only
1976	11,556	1,437	1,015	53	1,775
1977	7,296	616	1,145	48	2,385
1978	5,669	505	1,370	69	2,752
1979	4,889	424	1,931	99	3,148
1980	5,536	492	2,777	166	3,185
1981	6,057	659	3,095	193	3,204
1982	7,873	831	4,233	217	3,560
1983	8,490	728	4,903	313	3,173
1984	8,934	979	7,898	566	3,088
1985	10,561	1,225	9,403	615	3,329

Note: The ER data are based on 564 facilities that reported consistently throughout the 10-year period. The ME data are based on 62 facilities that reported consistently throughout the 10-year period.

Source: National Institute on Drug Abuse, Drug Abuse Warning Network (DAWN) historical data files as of August 1986.

Cocaine-related cases reported to DAWN seem to present a somewhat analogous enigma. The largest increases in the general prevalence of cocaine use occurred in the mid- to late 1970s. Yet, while the number of DAWN emergency room and medical examiner

[15]J. Colliver and J. Gampel, "A Decade of DAWN: Heroin-Related Cases, 1976-1985," unpublished paper prepared for the Division of Epidemiology and Statistical Analysis, National Institute on Drug Abuse, Rockville, Md., 1987.
[16]National Institute on Drug Abuse, *Demographic Characteristics and Patterns of Drug Use of Clients Admitted to Drug Abuse Treatment Programs in Selected States: Trend Data 1979-1984* (Washington, D.C.: U.S. Government Printing Office, 1988).

cases increased throughout the period between 1976 and 1985, the rate of increase accelerated in the 1980s as shown in table 4. Subsequent data for 1986 indicate additional very sharp increases midyear. So sharp, in fact, that by the second half of 1986, cocaine was the drug mentioned most frequently in DAWN emergency room cases.[17]

Treatment data, as an indicator of personal dysfunction, provide another measure of increasing adverse consequences associated with cocaine use. Between 1979 and 1984, the proportion of clients admitted for treatment of a primary cocaine problem increased from 3.9 percent to 14.7 percent.[18] These findings are based on data provided by a panel of 596 consistently reporting drug abuse treatment programs located in fifteen states.

While we speak of the "drug abuse problem," drug abuse is not, in fact, a singular phenomenon. The spread of drug problems and societal concern nationally appear to have shifted from marijuana in the 1960s to heroin in the 1970s to cocaine in the 1980s. The nature and extent of abuse varies by substance, time, demographic characteristics of users, and geographic region. In addition to these broad variations, the available data provide numerous insights into the many complexities and nuances of drug abuse epidemiology. The discussion which follows focuses on some of the special facets of drug abuse that are important for policy development and resource planning, and for targeting intervention and prevention activities.

FACTORS INFLUENCING OBSERVED DRUG ABUSE PATTERNS AND TRENDS

Heroin Use

Studies and investigations of heroin-related problems have shown that a number of factors influence trends reflected in the available data. As the concern of many in the field about heroin

---

[17]National Institute on Drug Abuse, *Semiannual Report Trend Data through July-December 1986*, Data from the Drug Abuse Warning Network, Statistical Series G, no. 19, DHHS Publication (ADM)87-1528 (Washington, D.C.: U.S. Government Printing Office, 1987).

[18]National Institute on Drug Abuse, *Cocaine Client Admissions 1979-1984*, DHHS Publication (ADM)87-1528 (Washington, D.C.: U.S. Government Printing Office, 1987).

lessened in the late 1970s, DAWN mortality data provided an early indication that a worsening heroin problem was developing in Washington, D.C. in mid-1979.[19] The resurgence of heroin-related problems, not only in Washington, but also in other northeastern areas between Washington and New York City, was quickly confirmed by other indicators such as treatment data, price and purity data, and reports from service providers and public officials in the affected areas.

An epidemiologic study of the heroin-related deaths in Washington, D.C. during the period 1979 to 1982 suggested that combining heroin use with ethanol ingestion, sporadic use of heroin, and the use of quinine as a diluent in the preparation of heroin were all contributing factors to the epidemic of heroin-related deaths in that city.[20] The increasing heroin-related morbidity shown in table 4 may, in part, reflect the use of multiple drugs. One study of those data found that the concomitant use of heroin and cocaine accounted for an increasing portion of all heroin-related cases.[21] The aging of the heroin-using population, which was noted earlier, might also be a factor in the increasing morbidity trends as the increasing years of exposure to heroin use and the associated life-style take their toll.

The price and purity of heroin are generally considered to be important indicators of the levels of heroin use, with the demand for heroin increasing as the price decreases and purity improves. Such changes have been cited as possible factors in the increasing heroin-related morbidity and mortality trends in areas outside the Northeast during the mid-1980s. Specifically, "black-tar" heroin, which is purported to be of relatively high purity and low price, became increasingly available in a number of areas throughout the country.[22]

---

[19]G.E. Powell, "Heroin Indicators in Washington, D.C.," in *Drug Abuse Indicator Trends*, Community Correspondents Group Proceedings, vol. 1, 1979, National Institute on Drug Abuse (Washington, D.C.: U.S. Government Printing Office, 1980).
[20]Centers for Disease Control, "Heroin-Related Deaths—District of Columbia, 1980-1982," *Morbidity and Mortality Weekly Report* 32 (1983):321-24; A.J. Ruttenber and J.L. Luke, "Heroin-Related Deaths: New Epidemiologic Insights," *Science* 226 (1984):14.
[21]J. Colliver and J. Gampel, "A Decade of DAWN: Heroin-Related Cases, 1976-1985."
[22]National Institute on Drug Abuse, *Drug Abuse Trends and Research Issues*, Community Epidemiology Work Group Proceedings, December 1986 (Washington, D.C.: U.S. Government Printing Office, 1987).

The types of factors cited as contributors to the observed heroin trends, such as user characteristics, localized problems, patterns of use, street product marketed, and multiple drug use, should also be considered in assessing trends for other drugs.

Cocaine Use

One of the major factors in the observed trend shown in table 4 for cocaine-related emergencies is the way users administer the drug. For that set of data, injection replaced sniffing as the most frequently reported route of administration of cocaine starting in 1983. At the same time, smoking, which had accounted for less than 2 percent of the cases prior to 1983, increased rapidly to 8 percent of the cases in 1985.[23] In a study of drug treatment admissions for cocaine problems, smoking as the client's most usual way of using cocaine increased from 1 percent in 1979 to 19 percent in 1984.[24]

During the late 1970s, freebase was introduced as a method to smoke cocaine. Cocaine base was processed from cocaine hydrochloride in a chemical process involving volatile chemicals, usually ether. In 1985, a new tactic was introduced in New York City for marketing cocaine on the street. This involved selling a freebase form called "crack." [25] Not only did "crack" facilitate the dangerous practice of smoking cocaine, it also made it easier for new populations of users to get involved with cocaine since it was sold in single 65-100 milligram doses for $10; by way of comparison, a typical gram lot of cocaine hydrochloride might cost $100.[26] "Crack" may be a primary factor in the increase cited earlier in cocaine-related hospital emergency room cases during 1986. About one in four of these cases during the latter part of 1986 involved smoking cocaine.

---

[23]J. Colliver, "A Decade of DAWN: Cocaine-Related Cases, 1976-1985," unpublished paper prepared for the Division of Epidemiology and Statistical Analysis, National Institute on Drug Abuse, Rockville, Md., 1987.
[24]National Institute on Drug Abuse, *National Household Survey on Drug Abuse.*
[25]B. Frank, W. Hopkins, and D.S. Lipton, "Drug Use Trends in New York City, December 1985," in *Epidemiology of Drug Abuse: Research*, Clinical and Social Perspectives, Community Epidemiology Work Group Proceedings, 1985, National Institute on Drug Abuse (Washington, D.C.: U.S. Government Printing Office, 1986); J.N. Hall, "Cocaine Smoking Ignites America," *Street Pharmacologist* 9:1 (1986).
[26]Kozel and Adams, "Epidemiology of Drug Abuse."

Geographic Variation

Table 3 suggests that while drug abuse may be prevalent in all regions of the country, there are geographic variations. Indeed, it is possible that particular abuse patterns may be prominent just in selected communities, or for that matter in a particular section of a community. For some drugs, such as cocaine and marijuana, use is widespread throughout the United States. Another major illicit drug, PCP, appears to have been a prominent problem primarily in the Los Angeles, New York City, and Washington, D.C. areas at least for the period mid-1970s to mid-1980s.[27] Variations in drug use patterns within communities have been reported by ethnographic researchers.[28]

Drug Combinations

Concomitant use of more than one drug is frequently implicated in adverse health consequences. In such cases, the user may be seeking the combined effect of both drugs. An example of this is the simultaneous injection of heroin and cocaine, a practice known as "speedballing." One particularly lethal combination, known as "Hits" or "Loads," involves the joint use of glutethimide and codeine—a practice that has been particularly problematic in New Jersey.[29]

During the late 1970s, a combination known as "T's and Blues" (pentazocine and tripelennamine) became a popular heroin substitute. The rise and decline in the popularity of this drug combination can be tracked in the DAWN data. Over the period 1976-1985, the number of pentazocine-related hospital emergency room cases increased from 800 in 1976 to a peak of 2,077 in 1981. By 1985, the number of cases plummeted to 542, reflecting the

---

[27]National Institute on Drug Abuse, *Trends in Drug Abuse Related Hospital Emergency Room Episodes and Medical Examiner Cases for Selected Drugs, DAWN 1976-1985,* Statistical Series H, no. 3, DHHS Publication (ADM)87-1524 (Washington, D.C.: U.S. Government Printing Office, 1987).

[28]D.S. Lipton, "Update of Major Drug Copping Areas in New York City," unpublished inter-office memorandum, New York State Division of Substance Abuse Services, July 19, 1983.

[29]E. Feuer, "The Epidemiology of Hits," in *Drug Abuse in Selected Metropolitan Areas—Reports on Trends and Lifestyles,* Community Correspondents Work Group Proceedings vol. 1, 1982, National Institute on Drug Abuse (Washington, D.C.: U.S. Government Printing Office, 1980).

manufacturer's reformulation of the product (trade name Talwin) with the addition of the opiate antagonist naloxone in December 1982.[30]

Gateway Drugs

Perhaps even more important than the concomitant use of multiple drugs are the long-term temporal relationships among drugs, including alcohol and cigarettes, the drugs most widely used for nonmedical purposes. While temporal relationships among drugs in initiation of their use do not indicate causality, they do suggest that once a threshold has been reached, the probability that another door may be opened increases.[31] It appears that there is a pattern of progression in the involvement of youth with drugs, which typically involves the use of alcohol and tobacco prior to the use of marijuana. Marijuana, in turn, is considered a "gateway" drug; few youths begin the use of other illicit drugs without first using marijuana. Frequent use of marijuana during adolescence has been found to be the best single predictor of cocaine use.[32] Both the frequency and recency of marijuana use increases the probability of cocaine use.[33]

Supply and Availability

The focus of this paper is on the demand side of the drug abuse equation. As indicated by the references to "black tar" heroin, the "crack" form of cocaine, and the reformulation of Talwin, however, the supply side cannot be ignored. Clearly, supply is an antece-

---

[30]National Institute on Drug Abuse, *Trends in Drug Abuse Related Hospital Emergency Room Episodes*.
[31]A.J. Blanken, E.H. Adams, and J. Durell, "Drug Abuse: Implications and Trends," *Psychiatric Medicine* 3:3 (1985):299-317.
[32]D.B. Kandel and R. Faust, "Sequence and States in Patterns of Adolescent Drug Use," *Archives of General Psychiatry* 32 (1975):923-932; R.R. Clayton and H.L. Voss, *Young Men and Drugs in Manhattan: A Causal Analysis*, NIDA Research Monograph, no. 39, DHHS Publication (ADM)81-1167 (Washington, D.C.: U.S. Government Printing Office, 1981); D.B. Kandel; D. Murphy; and D. Karus, "Cocaine Use in Young Adulthood: Patterns of Use and Psychosocial Correlates," in *Cocaine Use in America: Epidemiologic and Clinical Perspectives*, ed. N.J. Kozel and E.H. Adams, NIDA Research Monograph, no. 61, DHHS Publication (ADM)85-1414 (Washington, D.C.: U.S. Government Printing Office, 1985).
[33]E.H. Adams, J.C. Gfroerer, B.A. Rouse, and N.J. Kozel, "Trends in Prevalence and Consequences of Cocaine Use," *Advances in Alcohol and Substance Abuse* 6:2 (1986):49.

dent condition to abuse. The widespread and increasing use of methamphetamines observed in the San Diego area in the mid-1980s, for example, may be related to a glut of methamphetamines in the market; the glut, in turn, appears to be the result of over-production of the drug called "crystal meth," "speed," or "go fast" by clandestine laboratories.[34]

A special category of drugs officially called controlled substance analogues, but popularly referred to as "designer drugs," has caused increasing concern during the 1980s. These drugs are chemically and pharmacologically similar to substances listed in the Controlled Substance Act but were not themselves controlled until the passage of the Controlled Substance Analog Enforcement Act of 1986. Examples include 3-methylfentanyl, a narcotic analogue, and MDMA (called "Ecstasy" or "XTC"), a neurotoxic analogue of MDA and methamphetamine. Compared to other abused substances, levels of use of these drugs are apparently low; however, the potential of serious adverse consequences for users of some of these clandestinely produced substances is great.[35] Some of the fentanyl analogues are as much as several thousand times more potent than morphine.

Street drugs, whether manufactured in local clandestine laboratories or imported through illicit drug trafficking channels, are essentially an unknown quantity to the user—in terms of dosage, purity, and, for that matter, actual content. One analysis of drugs tested in 1983 by an anonymous testing service indicated that buyers frequently did not obtain the drug they thought they were buying. For example, the validity rate (i.e., the drug contained in the sample was the same as alleged) was only 6 percent for amphetamines and 37 percent for methamphetamines. When the alleged drug plus adulterants were considered, the methamphetamine rate was 95 percent; the amphetamine rate, however, remained low at 17 percent. Most amphetamine samples contained caffeine, ephedrine and phenylpropanolamine.[36] Thus, in addition to the potential of being "ripped off," the street drug customer is subjecting himself/herself to risks of using unknown substances.

---

[34]National Institute on Drug Abuse, *Drug Abuse Trends and Research Issues*.
[35]National Narcotics Intelligence Consumers Committee, *The NNICC Report 1985-1986*.
[36]Renfroe, ed., "The 1983 Drug Analysis Results," *Pharm Chem Newsletter* 13:(1984).

While supply is necessary, data from the High School Senior Survey indicate that trends in drug use are not simply artifacts of availability.[37] As current (past month) use of marijuana declined from 37 percent in 1978 to 23 percent in 1986, most seniors (85 percent in 1986 compared to 88 percent in 1978) continued to report that it would be "fairly easy" or "very easy" to get marijuana if they wanted some (table 5). Over the same time period, the percent saying they thought there was a great risk of harm in regularly smoking marijuana doubled—from 35 percent to 71 percent. In 1978, 35 percent of the students estimated that most or all of their friends smoked marijuana compared to 18 percent in 1986. These data appear to indicate that high school seniors are increasingly concerned about their health while, at the same time, the social milieu is less conducive to using marijuana.

Table 5. Trends in Prevalence, Reported Availability, Perceived Harm, and Friends' Use of Marijuana among United States High School Seniors: 1976-1986

	1976	1978	1980	1982	1984	1986
Marijuana						
Prevalence:						
Used in Past Month	32.2%	37.1%	33.7%	28.5%	25.2%	23.4%
Used Daily in Past Month	8.2	10.7	9.1	6.3	5.0	4.0
Reported Availability:						
Percent saying it would be "fairly easy" or "very easy" to get marijuana	87.4	87.8	89.0	88.5	84.6	85.2
Perceived Harm:						
Percent saying they think there is "great risk" of harm in smoking marijuana regularly	38.6	34.9	50.4	60.4	66.9	71.3
Friends' Use:						
Percent saying "most or all" of their friends smoke marijuana	30.6	35.3	31.3	23.8	18.3	18.2

Source: National Institute on Drug Abuse, High School Senior Survey.

[37]L.D. Johnston, P.M. O'Malley, and J.G. Bachman, *National Trends in Drug Use and Related Factors among American High School Students and Young Adults 1975-1986*, DHHS Publication (ADM)87-1535 (Washington, D.C.: U.S. Government Printing Office, 1987).

In summary, studies that have focused on particular drug abuse phenomena underscore the dynamic and diverse nature of factors contributing to the drug abuse problem in the United States. A recognition that drug abuse is indeed a complex and many-faceted problem is critical to the development of solutions.

DISCUSSION

While Freud sang the praises of cocaine, Erlenmeyer attacked Freud for unleashing the third scourge of humanity (after alcohol and morphine). Nearly a century later, the second report from the National Commission on Marihuana and Drug Abuse stated that little social cost related to cocaine had been verified in this country.[38] At the same time, the Strategy Council on Drug Abuse stated that morbidity associated with cocaine use did not appear to be great.[39] By 1986, more than 1,000 cocaine-related deaths and nearly 25,000 cocaine-related emergency room visits were reported through the DAWN system.[40] Not only does it appear that drug abuse problems become manifest in a society in waves and cycles over time, but also that society must learn and relearn the potential dangers associated with such use. This underscores the importance of continuing scientific research designed to increase knowledge of the pharmacologic action of drugs in the body, describe the etiology of drug abuse, identify risk factors for initiation to drug use, quantify the nature and extent of the problem, monitor changes over time, and identify the short- and long-term consequences of use of specific drugs.

The available epidemiologic data indicate that drug use in the United States remains a major social problem; it is pervasive in extent, diverse in its manifestations, and constantly changing. While historic patterns may repeat themselves in a general sense, drug abuse in the United States in the 1980s is unique both in the magnitude of spread to various segments of the population and in the

---

[38]National Commission on Marihuana and Drug Abuse, *Drug Use in America: Problem in Perspective*, Second report of the National Commission on Marihuana and Drug Abuse (Washington, D.C.: U.S. Government Printing Office, 1973).
[39]Strategy Council on Drug Abuse, *Federal Strategy for Drug Abuse and Drug Traffic Prevention 1973* (Washington, D.C.: U.S. Government Printing Office, 1973).
[40]National Institute on Drug Abuse, *Annual Data 1986, Data from the Drug Abuse Warning Network*, Statistical Series I, no. 6, DHHS Publication (ADM)87-1530 (Washington, D.C.: U.S. Government Printing Office, 1987).

number and combinations of substances abused. Gathering accurate data about the size of the problem, the type of people involved, and the drugs being abused is the first task in breaking the cycle of drug abuse.

Measurement of drug abuse is complicated by the fact that drug abuse is an illicit behavior. Additionally, populations with disproportionately high levels of drug abuse, such as persons without a fixed address, will not be included in the sampling universe for traditional survey methodologies. Thus, measurements of the demand for illicit drugs must generally be viewed as conservative estimates.

Definitional constraints may hinder proper identification of drug abuse problems. The term "addiction" used to be restricted to the physical withdrawal symptoms resulting from opiate and depressant dependence. The compulsive drug-seeking behavior associated with cocaine abuse has necessitated a change in that definition.

In a health care setting the overt medical complaints, e.g., accidental trauma, may obscure an underlying drug abuse problem. Phencyclidine (PCP) reactions may appear as psychiatric emergencies, often misdiagnosed as schizophrenia because the patient suffers from paranoid symptoms, hostility, confusion, and a tendency toward violent and extremely unpredictable behavior.

The complexities of assessing the nature of drug abuse problems are further exacerbated by the range of drugs and other chemical substances abused, how they are combined, and how they are used. The havoc created in areas like New York City and Miami when the base form of cocaine called "crack" was introduced in the street market illustrates how an already serious problem increased exponentially because of the apparent widespread adoption of smoking as the preferred way to administer cocaine. While the popularity of specific drug combinations may wane or grow over time, new ones are continually being added.

As drugs and patterns of use vary, so do the social and health consequences to the user. It is, of course, these adverse consequences to society as a whole, as well as to the individual user, that make drug abuse such a serious national problem. The widespread prevalence of marijuana use and possible detrimental consequences for adolescent development have serious implications for the future. Numerous clinical effects, e.g., impaired lung function, have also been associated with marijuana use.[41] Concern about the cardiovascular risks associated with cocaine use has increased as a result of reports of cocaine-related heart attacks in relatively healthy individuals.[42] Intravenous drug abusers are at high risk for contracting acquired immune deficiency syndrome (AIDS) as well as numerous other diseases.

Prevention and intervention programs designed to address problems associated with drug abuse must consider differences and diversity in underlying motivation for initial use, in user populations, in classes of drugs used, in adverse consequences, and in effective treatment approaches. Long after the spread of drug abuse recedes, the aftermath of the epidemic will be felt by users experiencing problems associated with dependency and chronic effects, by the service delivery system as demand for treatment continues, and by society as a whole as it attempts to protect its young through education and prevention activities. In the long term, solutions depend on research and on continuing commitment to addressing the many and varied facets of "the drug abuse problem."

---

[41]Institute of Medicine, *Marijuana and Health; Report of a Study by a Committee of the Institute of Medicine* (Washington, D.C.: National Academy Press, 1982).

[42]R.E. Howard, D.C. Jeuter, and G.J. Davis, "Acute Myocardial Infarction following Cocaine Abuse in a Young Woman with Normal Coronary Arteries," *Journal of the American Medical Association* 254:1 (1985):95; P.F. Pasternack; S.B. Colvin; and F.G. Bauman, "Cocaine-Induced Angina Pectoris and Acute Myocardial Infarction in Patients Younger than 40 Years," *American Journal of Cardiology* 55 (1985):847; L.C. Cregler and H. Mark, "Relation of Acute Myocardial Infarction to Cocaine Abuse," *American Journal of Cardiology* 56 (1985):794.

APPENDIX—NATIONAL DATA
COLLECTION SYSTEM

National Household Survey on Drug Abuse

A sample survey of persons aged twelve years and older in the general household population of the coterminous United States. Information is obtained on the prevalence of illicit drug use through personal interview combined with private answer sheets. It was conducted every two or three years between 1972 and 1985 (N=8,038). Beginning with the 1988 survey, it will be conducted biennially.

High School Senior Survey

A sample survey of approximately 16,000 seniors in public and private high schools, conducted annually since 1975. Information is collected on the prevalence of and attitudes toward illicit drug use through self-administered questionnaires.

The prevalence measures derived from both the National Household Survey and the High School Senior Survey include: ever use (or lifetime prevalence) which reflects use on at least one occasion in a person's lifetime; and past month use (or current use) which reflects use at least once in the thirty days prior to interview.

Drug Abuse Warning Network (DAWN)

An ongoing data collection system which collects patient characteristic and drug use data on drug abuse-related hospital emergency room (ER) and medical examiner (ME) cases. Implemented in 1973, DAWN collects data from a nonrandom sample of over 700 ERs and 70 MEs located primarily in twenty-seven metropolitan areas throughout the country. In DAWN, specific drug types (not just classes of drugs) are reported.

Treatment Client Data

Prior to the implementation of the Block Grant (to states) program for federal alcohol, drug abuse, and mental health treatment funds in 1981, the National Institute on Drug Abuse (NIDA) required reporting on all clients admitted to treatment in federally funded drug abuse treatment programs. Since 1982, a number of states have continued to operate their own treatment client data systems and have shared these data with NIDA. For that subpopulation of users who seek treatment, these data provide information on client characteristics, type of treatment admitted to, and drug use patterns.

3

Mexico's Changing Illicit Drug Supply Role

Miguel Ruiz-Cabañas I.

The phenomena of cultivation, production, trafficking, and consumption of illicit drugs have reached global proportions. The International Narcotics Control Board (INCB) stated in its 1986 report that these illicit activities are now taking place in every region of the world and that the abuse of both natural and synthetic drugs has spread so that it affects "virtually all countries, and menaces all segments of society, including young persons and even children."[1] According to this report, however, there are some countries where the magnitude of the phenomena associated with drug production or abuse is so great as to deserve special attention: in North America, Canada, the United States, and Mexico; Jamaica and the Bahamas in the Caribbean; in South America, Colombia, Bolivia, Peru, Ecuador, and Brazil; in Southwest Asia, Afghanistan, Iran, and Pakistan; the Southeast Asia region—Burma, Thailand, India, the Lao People's Democratic Republic, and Malaysia; and most countries of Western Europe.[2]

The cultivation of cannabis in Mexico can be traced to at least the nineteenth century. It has been available in the United States since the first decade of this century.[3] The illicit production of

---

[1] See *Report of the International Narcotics Control Board (INCB) for 1986*, U.N. document E/INCB/1986/1, p. 3.
[2] Ibid., pp. 3-7.
[3] See William O. Walker, *Drug Control in the Americas* (Albuquerque: University of New Mexico Press, 1981), pp. 1-23.

opium, which apparently was introduced in the twenties,[4] boomed
in the early seventies when Mexican supply replaced the Turkish
supply for the U.S. market.[5] There is no cultivation of coca leaves
in Mexico, but the country has become an important transit point
for this South American-produced drug since the U.S. demand for
and consumption of cocaine soared in the early seventies.[6]

The cultivation and production of illicit drugs in Mexico for
consumption in the United States has been a significant source of
problems and diplomatic frictions between the two neighbors since
the 1930s. It has been particularly so during the last twenty years.
Few other problems, if any, have shown a greater potential to
drastically deteriorate the U.S.-Mexican relation. The trafficking of
illicit drugs can poison many other aspects of the bilateral relation by contaminating the negotiating climate for important commercial, financial, or migration problems. Its mere presence tends
to relegate other problems to a secondary position on the bilateral
agenda.[7]

The supply of illicit drugs to the U.S. market comes from many
sources. Mexico is an important source of supply, and practically
all Mexican export production of illicit drugs goes to the United
States. With the possible exception of heroin in Canada,[8] there are
no reports of important quantities of Mexican drugs seized in other
countries. The real dimensions of the Mexican supply of illicit drugs
are practically unknowable. There are no reliable statistics, and the
illicit nature of the activity means that the most sophisticated figure can only be an estimate.[9] Nevertheless, we must analyze its
approximate dimensions and major characteristics if we want to

---

[4]Ibid., p. 167.
[5]See President's Commission on Organized Crime, Report to the President and
Attorney General, *America's Habit: Drug Abuse, Drug Trafficking and Organized Crime*
(Washington, D.C.: U.S. Government Printing Office, 1986), pp. 107-110.
[6]See Procuraduría General de la República (Supervisión General de Servicios Técnicos y Criminalísticos), *El esfuerzo de México. Campaña permanente contra el narcotráfico,
1986* (México, D.F.: Talleres Gráficos de la Nación, 1987), pp. 47-76. See also,
President's Commission on Organized Crime, *America's Habit*, pp. 73-104.
[7]For an analysis of recent disputes between the two countries see Guadalupe
González, "El problema del narcotráfico en el contexto de la relación entre México
y Estados Unidos," in *Carta de Política Exterior Mexicana* (CIDE) 5:2-3 (April-
September 1985):20-28.
[8]See the *Annual Reports* of the INCB.
[9]See the *International Narcotics Control Strategy Report* (annual reports of the U.S.
Department of State Bureau of International Narcotics Matters), or *The Supply of
Illicit Drugs to the United States from Foreign and Domestic Sources (With Near Term
Projections)* (annual reports of the National Narcotics Intelligence Consumers
Committee [NNICC]).

understand the problem of drug trafficking between the two nations. The significance of the Mexican supply of illicit drugs to the United States, however, can only be appreciated by first placing it in the proper framework: the global supply of illicit drugs to the U.S. market. We also have to analyze it in relation to demand and consumption in Mexico, keeping in mind the fundamental economic principle that "where a demand for a service or commodity exists, some entrepreneur, for the right price, will attempt to supply it."[10]

In light of these considerations this paper aims to describe the changing role of the Mexican supply of illicit drugs to the United States and its interactions with other sources of supply, and to suggest some perspectives for the future on the possible role of the Mexican supply.

PROBLEMS WITH DATA

The first problem we confront in calculating the Mexican share of the supply of illicit drugs to the United States is the lack of data. The cultivation, manufacture, and commercialization of illicit drugs is by definition an illegal activity. Producers, exporters/importers, wholesalers, dealers, and "pushers" do not report to the governments on their activities, nor do they pay taxes. There are only two available sources of data, both produced and published by U.S. government agencies: the annual *International Narcotics Control Strategy Report* (INCSR), produced by the Bureau of International Narcotics Matters of the Department of State, and the annual report of the National Narcotics Intelligence Consumers Committee (NNICC).[11]

---

[10]President's Commission on Organized Crime, *America's Habit*, p. 237.

[11]In the preface to its reports the NNICC informs us that most of its figures are derived from law enforcement activities and therefore "cannot be used by themselves as a basis for estimates of quantities of drugs available or consumed. Because of gaps in some of the data used to derive the estimates, there is a high degree of uncertainty to the resulting estimates. It is believed, however, that they are sufficiently accurate that the general trends portrayed can be considered to be reliable."

There are, however, some methodological problems in the preparation of these data that should be noted. We can offer two examples: 1) the estimates on drug cultivation and production of the U.S. Department of State; 2) the NNICC estimates are, as explicitly stated in its 1987 *Report*, an "attempt to show *actual production or net yield, subtracting for eradication*." Thus, their figures are stated "post-eradication, and the totals have not been discounted for losses, domestic consumption or seizures." (The estimates, however, are provided in metric tons, and not in the

The preparation of the data in these reports presents some methodological problems, the most important of which, as Mark Kleiman has said, is that "they are presented as just a set of conclusions, without any detailed presentation of the underlying data or the calculations performed on the data."[12] We have used these sources in this section, in spite of their limitations, because of the lack of other systematic statistics. We have used data from other sources in those cases where they are available.

---

extension of land cultivated, which implies the use of a yield factor.) In the last INCSR *Report*, it was assumed that Mexican production of marijuana in 1986 was around four to six thousand metric tons. Despite the admission that losses, domestic consumption, and seizures had not been discounted, the assumption for Mexican production does not change when the same report makes a net estimate of marijuana available in the U.S. market: four to six thousand metric tons.. The problem with this method is that it ignores a fundamental fact that has been highlighted by Mark Kleiman: A large part of the total crop may go unsold in every country where drugs are produced. It is conceivable that a peasant will try to "overproduce" to guarantee a minimum sale every year. But this does not mean that the entire crop was available for the U.S. market. The same problem affects the NNICC, leading Kleiman to explain that "The crop figures themselves are hard to distinguish from guesswork, and the fraction of each country's crop reaching the U.S. market is fundamentally unknown."

In its 1983 report, the NNICC presumed that total marijuana consumption in the United States in 1982 had been in the range of 12,340 to 14,040 metric tons, which would represent a 12 percent increase from 1981. In the 1984 report, however, the marijuana consumption estimate for 1982 was lowered to 8,200-10,200 metric tons, which would represent a decrease of 5 percent compared with 1981. Moreover, in its last report, which covers 1985-1986, the NNICC offers a new and significantly lower estimate of marijuana consumption for 1982, of only 4,899.8 metric tons. According to this report, total consumption in 1985 did not exceed 4,693.9 metric tons. In the same report, however, we are informed that there has been a trend to an increased number of hospital emergencies related to marijuana consumption: 3,360, 3,317, 3,710, and 4,201 in 1983, 1984, 1985, and 1986, respectively.

There are two problems with these estimates and reviews of the estimates: First, it is explained that new data and new methodologies provided the basis for the reviews on the total consumption, but we are not explicitly told which new data or methodologies were introduced to permit these new estimates; second, there is an inconsistency between the trend to report lower levels of consumption among the population on the one hand, and the trend to present more hospital emergencies related to marijuana consumption on the other. Since the latter could be the result of inadequacies in the current method used by the NNICC to estimate the consumption of illicit drugs among the population, so tending to underestimate the consumption of the "heavy users," we cannot be sure that the new figures are more reliable.

[12]See Mark Kleiman, "Data and Analysis Requirements for Policy toward Drug Enforcement and Organized Crime," in President's Commission on Organized Crime, *America's Habit*, Appendix G, p. 59.

THE MEXICAN SUPPLY OF CANNABIS

The cultivation and production of cannabis in Mexico can be traced at least to the last century. Then, as in the first decades of this century, cannabis was viewed more as a useful substance with medical and other applications than as a drug. Concerned about spreading drug abuse, however, the Mexican government prohibited marijuana cultivation in 1923 and in 1927 banned its export.[13]

Records show that Mexican marijuana has been exported to the United States since the nineteenth century. Marijuana was also produced in the United States, where some of the same positive views prevailed as to its usefulness. Although its consumption as a drug was associated with racial minorities, Mexican-Americans in particular, it was not generally regarded as a dangerous drug before the adoption in the 1920s of several laws practically prohibiting its use. This restrictive movement peaked with the adoption of the Marijuana Tax Act in 1937. These laws did not eliminate marijuana trafficking in the United States, however, and the supply and consumption of the drug continued unabated in the 1930s and 1940s, causing occasional diplomatic friction between the two neighbors. This continued in the 1950s and early 1960s without being regarded as a particularly grave problem, perhaps because marijuana use was continuously associated with minorities.[14]

The widespread increases in consumption that took place among the young U.S. population in the late sixties radically altered public and official perceptions of drug abuse, in particular of Mexican marijuana. In 1969, the then-new Nixon administration launched "Operation Intercept." Conceived as a major interagency interdiction attempt along the Mexican border, Operation Intercept resulted in far fewer seizures than expected and caused serious strains in the U.S. relationship with Mexico. It was later transformed into "Operation Cooperation," which included Mexican government participation in interdiction efforts.[15]

---

[13]See Walker, *Drug Control*, pp. 48-49.
[14]For a short history of marijuana laws in the United States, see Jerome L. Himmelstein, *The Strange Career of Marijuana: Politics and Ideology of Drug Control in America* (Westport, Conn: Greenwood Press, 1983). See also, President's Commission on Organized Crime, *America's Habit*, pp. 187-223.
[15]See Walker, *Drug Control*, pp. 153-181. See also Richard Craig, "Operación Intercepción: una política de presión internacional," *Foro Internacional* 86:22(2) (October-December 1981).

In 1975 Mexico substantially increased its interdiction efforts and reinforced an eradication campaign that remains in force today. Mexico eradicated more than 5,900 hectares of cannabis cultivation from 1977 to 1979,[16] reducing the supply of Mexican marijuana in the United States from more than 75 percent in 1976 to around 11 percent in 1979.[17] This decreasing trend continued until 1981, when the estimated share of Mexican marijuana available in the United States was only 4 percent of the entire supply. Low levels of supply of Mexican marijuana in the United States were maintained in 1982 (6 percent) and 1983 (9 percent). Table 1 presents the NNICC estimates on production and participation in the U.S. market of Mexican marijuana for the years 1979-83.

Table 1. Mexico: NNICC Estimates on Marijuana Production and Participation in the U.S. Market

	1979	1980	1981	1982	1983
Production (tons)	1100-1500	800-1300	300-500	750	1300
U.S. supply (percent)	11	8	4	6	9
Eradication (hectares)	657	699	508	850	2600

Source: NNICC *Reports* 1980 and 1983. Figures on eradication were obtained from the United Nations *Review of the Illicit Traffic in Narcotic Drugs and Psychotropic Substances* (several years) Part II. Statistical Tables of Drugs Seized, U.N. document E/CN.7/1985/CRP.11, E/CN.7/1983/10 (part 2).

The substantial reductions in the Mexican supply of the late 1970s and early 1980s left a vacuum that was rapidly filled by marijuana produced in Colombia and by domestic U.S. production. Jamaican and other sources also reemerged significantly to contribute to satisfaction of the growing demand. The increased production and participation of these three sources can be seen in table 2.

Kleiman affirms that the NNICC figures are hard to distinguish from "guesswork," and that the fraction of each country's crop reaching the U.S. market is fundamentally unknown.[18] Even if we regard these estimates as mere guesses, however, the trends they

[16]Data obtained from the United Nations Economic and Social Council Commission on Narcotics, *Review of the Illicit Traffic in Narcotic Drugs and Psychotropic Substances during 1979: Statistical Tables of Drugs Seized* (part II), U.N. document E/CN.7/641.
[17]See the 1980 NNICC *Report*, p. 54
[18]Kleiman, "Data and Analysis Requirements," p. 56.

Table 2. Marijuana Production and Participation in the U.S. Market

	1979	1980	1981	1982	1983
Colombia					
Production	7450-	7700-	7500-	7000-	6900-
(tons)	10000	11000	11000	8000	9300
U.S. supply					
(percent)	75	75	79	57	57
United States					
Production	700-	700-	400-	2000	2000
(tons)	1000	1000	1200	—	—
U.S. supply					
(percent)	7	7	9	15	14
Jamaica					
Production	750-	1000-	400-	1750-	1750
(tons)	1000	1400	1200	2500	—
U.S. supply					
(percent)	7	10	9	16	12
Other					
Production	—	—	—	840	1150
(tons)	—	—	—	—	—
U.S. supply					
(percent)	—	—	—	6	8

Source: NNICC *Reports*, 1980 and 1983.

show are very clear. The near-total elimination of the Mexican supply of cannabis did not produce a near-total elimination of marijuana consumption in the United States. The reduced Mexican supply was substituted by other sources which responded to the growing U.S. consumption in the late 1970s. Thus, according to the estimates of the National Institute on Drug Abuse (NIDA), in 1972, 14 percent of twelve- to seventeen-year-olds, 47 percent of the population between eighteen and twenty-five, and 7.4 percent of those older than twenty-six had used marijuana at least once in the previous year. By 1979 these proportions had reached 30.9 percent, 68 percent, and 19.6 percent.[19]

The NNICC considers that there has been a continuous increase in the Mexican supply of cannabis to the United States since its 1983 level of 9 percent of the total. It was estimated at 20 percent in 1984 and 32 percent in 1985. In 1986 it was estimated at 30 percent, a slight decline. Estimates on production and participation of Mexican and other sources of cannabis supply to the United States since 1983 appear in table 3.

---

[19]See U.S. Department of Health and Human Services, National Institute on Drug Abuse, *National Survey on Drug Abuse: Main Findings 1982*, tables 5, 6, and 7, pp. 16-18.

Table 3. Marijuana Available in the U.S. by Source

	1983	1984	1985	1986
Mexico				
Production	1300	2500-	3000-	3000-
(tons)	—	3000	4000	4000
% U.S. supply	9	20	32	30
Colombia				
Production	6900-	4100-	2600-	2200-
(tons)	9300	7500	4000	3900
% U.S. supply	57	42	31	17
United States	2000	1700	2100	2100
Production				
(tons)				
% U.S. supply	14	12	19	18
Jamaica				
Production	1750	1500-	350-	1100-
(tons)	—	2250	850	1700
% U.S. supply	12	14	6	12
Belize				
Production	—	1100	550	500
(tons)				
% U.S. supply	—	8	5	4
Other				
Production	1150	500	800	800
(tons)				
% U.S. supply	8	4	7	8
TOTAL	13200-	11400-	9400-	9700-
	15500	16050	12300	13400
Less seizures	4490-	4120-	3000-	3000-
and losses	5090	5290	4000	4000
Net marijuana	8610-	7280-	6400-	6700-
available	10410	10760	8300	9400

Source: NNICC, *Reports* 1984 and 1985-1986.

According to the NNICC, the Colombian government has reduced substantially the production of cannabis in that country, therefore reducing its participation in the U.S. market from 57 percent in 1983 to 27 percent in 1986. The gains made in these years in Colombia, however, have been "partially offset by increasing availability of Mexican, Jamaican, and domestically grown supplies."[20] The data presented in table 3 indicate that U.S. domestic production of marijuana has remained nearly constant over the last four years—approximately 2.1 thousand metric tons—but the domestic share of total supply increased from 14 percent in 1983 to 18 percent in 1986 due to important reductions in supply from

---

[20]See the 1985-86 NNICC *Report*, p. 9.

other sources. Jamaica has remained an important supplier of cannabis to the United States, with more than 12 percent of the market in 1986, in spite of some production reductions in 1985, and Belize has emerged in the last three years as another important supplier of marijuana to the United States even though it shows a trend toward decreasing production as well.

It is impossible to directly prove or disprove the accuracy of the data in these reports. We will therefore concentrate our attention on some of the problems that arise when they are compared with other data from consumption trends surveys.

The NNICC has revised its estimates on the total amount of marijuana consumed in the United States during 1982 and 1985 (revised data for other years are not yet available). The new estimate for 1982 is 4899 metric tons (m.t.), and 4693.9 m.t. for 1985. If these are accurate and considering that the total amount of marijuana available in the United States in 1985 has been estimated at around 6400 to 8300 m.t., then there was a minimum of 1700 m.t. to a maximum of 3600 m.t. of marijuana available in the United States that was not consumed. This possibility seems very unlikely, but it is not unthinkable. The question becomes more complicated, however, when we are informed by the same report that prices for different varieties of cannabis remained stable or even increased in 1985.[21]

There is a widening gap between estimates of foreign production and supply of marijuana to the United States and of internal demand and consumption. There is no clear or easy explanation for this, but at least one conclusion seems inevitable: If the amount of marijuana consumed in the last four years was substantially less than previously estimated, then the estimates of foreign production and supply should be revised accordingly. It is inconceivable that prices remained stable in the face of increasing production and availability alongside decreasing demand and consumption. The NNICC estimates nonetheless make it clear that whenever the flow of cannabis from a foreign source has been substantially reduced, without similar reduction of the demand and consumption in the United States, the resulting shortage has been rapidly filled from other sources. As stated in the report of the Commission on Organized Crime, established by President Reagan:

---

[21]Ibid., figure 4.

> This short history of marijuana trafficking demon-
> strates that law enforcement pressure in a particu-
> lar cultivation area is compensated by production
> and trafficking increases elsewhere.[22]

This is also true in the United States, as indirectly evidenced by the growing number of plants destroyed there. According to the Drug Enforcement Administration, 12.9 million cannabis plants were eradicated, 649 greenhouse/indoor operations were seized, and 4,941 persons were arrested in 1984. In 1985, 39.2 million plants were eradicated, 951 indoor facilities were seized, and 5,151 persons were arrested; 129.6 million plants were eradicated in 1986 (ten times more than in 1984), along with 1,077 indoor facilities seized and 5,537 persons arrested.[23] The effectiveness of this eradication program in comparison with other such programs cannot be assessed, however, because there is no information on the amount in metric tons of plants destroyed, nor is there any estimate of total U.S. marijuana production.

THE MEXICAN SUPPLY OF OPIUM AND HEROIN

Opium cultivation and production in Mexico apparently began in the early 1920s in the states of Sonora, Sinaloa, Chihuahua, and Durango. The federal government banned its production almost immediately, in 1925, and adopted several legal sanctions against both sellers and users. As in the case of marijuana, in 1927 President Plutarco Elías Calles signed a decree prohibiting the export of opium. Moreover, in 1929 the provisions of a revised penal code included strict penalties against drug growers, producers, and traffickers.[24] Since then, with the exception of a brief three-month period in 1940, these activities have been illegal in Mexico.[25]

Opium use has been recorded in the United States since the second half of the last century. However, starting in 1875, when the city of San Francisco prohibited opium smoking Chinese dens—and especially after the adoption of the Harrison Act in 1914, whose stated purpose was to regulate the production and trade of opium—the United States adopted increasingly restrictive policies for

---

[22]See President's Commission on Organized Crime, *America's Habit*, p. 154.
[23]See National Drug Policy Board, *Federal Drug Enforcement Progress Report, 1986* (Washington, D.C.: U.S. Government Printing Office, 1987), Exhibit V-I, p. 104.
[24]See Walker, *Drug Control*, pp. 48-49.
[25]Ibid., pp. 119-133.

controlling the trade and illicit consumption of opium and its derivatives, morphine and heroin.[26]

Opium smoking gradually decreased in the United States but was replaced by a continuous increase in heroin abuse. During the 1920s and 1930s the bulk of the imported opium came from Italy, France, Asia, and the Mideast, and internal trade in the drug was controlled by several Mafia organizations based in New York City. The Mexican supply of heroin during this period apparently was not more than 10 to 15 percent of the total, but its share increased substantially when the European and Asian sources became inaccessible during World War II. After the war, however, La Cosa Nostra regained control of heroin imports from Italian sources. When the Italian government prohibited the manufacture of heroin in 1952, the Mafia replaced this supply with Turkish morphine that was usually transformed into heroin in the French city of Marseilles.[27]

According to U.S. Congress estimates, during the 1950s and 1960s the Mexican heroin supply was not more than 10 to 15 percent.[28] The Turkish government banned the production of opium in July 1972, however, and the supply from Mexico increased substantially. A few months after the Turkish-French heroin supply was cut off, "it was discovered that relatively small quantities of Mexican type heroin were being sold in a number of cities wherein it had not previous appeared,"[29] such as Washington, Philadelphia, Miami, and New York. From 1972 to 1975 the supply of heroin from Mexico increased from 10-15 percent to 80 percent of the total supply, calculated at more than six metric tons.[30] The Mexican supply literally replaced Turkish-European heroin within three years.

---

[26]See President's Commission on Organized Crime, *America's Habit*, pp. 188-205. The principle that the use of opiates (and later other drugs) should be restricted to medical and scientific purposes was established at that time. Since then the U.S. government has launched many international initiatives, both bilateral—with countries like Mexico—and multilateral—in the framework of the League of Nations (despite its formal absence from the organization)—to promote this principle. These attempts were generally highly successful, and this principle still governs international cooperation in the area of drugs.

[27]Ibid., pp. 105-132.

[28]See Morgan Murphy and Robert H. Steele, *The World Narcotics Problem: The Latin American Perspective. Report of Special Study Mission to Latin America and the Federal Republic of Germany*, 93rd Congress, Committee on Foreign Affairs (Washington, D.C.: U.S. Government Printing Office, 1973), p. 14.

[29]Ibid., p. 16.

[30]See President's Commission on Organized Crime, *America's Habit*, p. 106.

Faced with this situation, Mexico radically stepped up its poppy cultivation eradication efforts. In 1976, the government reported the destruction of 3,571 hectares of opium poppies. The eradication campaign has continued since then with the cooperation and assistance of the U.S. government. The efforts were successful according to NNICC estimates in that the participation of the Mexican supply to the United States was reduced from 67 percent in 1976 to 25 percent in 1980. Estimates of total Mexican opium production, relative participation in the U.S. market, and hectares eradicated can be seen in table 4.

Table 4. Mexican Opium Production, Participation in the U.S. Market, and Eradication, 1976-1980

	1976	1977	1978	1979	1980
Production estimate (m.t.)	40	30	20	9-12	17
Participation in U.S. supply (%)	67	56	44	30	25
Eradication (ha)*	3 571	8 957	1 781	7 461	1 625

Source: NNICC, *Report*, 1980.

*Figures from eradication were obtained from the United Nations, *Review of the Illicit Traffic in Narcotic Drugs and Psychotropic Substances* (several years) *Part II, Statistical Tables of Drugs Seized*, U.N. document E/CN.7/1985/CRP.11, E/CN.7/1983/10.

Table 4 shows how the eradication program achieved positive results. Estimated production for 1979 was reduced to one-third of what it was in 1976. It is believed that an increase in production occurred in 1980, but Mexican participation in the total supply that year was still only 25 percent.

The eradication campaign and reductions in the Mexican heroin supply were appreciated by the U.S. government. In its 1980 report, the NNICC stated:

> Mexico remains a bright spot in an otherwise discouraging crop eradication picture. A total of 3,620 acres of poppies were destroyed in 1980, double the average of previous years. The eradication effort in 1980 accounted for about 60 percent of the total cultivated area on the assumption that all the poppy plants were destroyed prior to extracting the opium gum.[31]

---

[31] 1980 NNICC *Report*, p. 91.

The reduction of the Mexican heroin supply was not accompanied by a similar trend in U.S. consumption. A new source of supply—this time from Southwest Asia (Afghanistan, Iran, Pakistan)—replaced the Mexican supply, as shown in table 5.

Table 5. Estimates on Heroin Available in the U.S. by Source of Origin

	1976	1977	1978	1979	1980
SW Asia	0	0.4*	0.8	1.3-1.5	2.2-2.6
	—	7%	18%	38%	60%
SE Asia	2.0	2.0	1.7	1.1-1.3	0.5-0.7
	33%	37%	38%	32%	15%
Mexico	4.0	3.0	2.0	1.0-1.2	0.9-1.0
	67%	56%	44%	30%	25%
U.S. addicts	560,000	495,000	470,000	420,000	450,000

*Amounts are given in metric tons.
Source: NNICC *Reports*, 1980.

Table 5 shows how the supply of heroin from Southwest Asia increased from zero in 1976 to 2.2-2.6 metric tons in 1980, equivalent to 60 percent of the total supply. The table also shows how the trend toward reduced consumption was less significant, with the number of addicts falling from an estimated 520,000 in 1976 to some 450,000 in 1980. Moreover, a new survey in 1981 estimated the U.S. population of heroin addicts at 492,000.[32]

The NNICC estimates indicate a continuous increase in opium and heroin production in Mexico since 1981, particularly after 1984. The participation of the Mexican heroin supply would thus have increased from an estimated 1.6 m.t. in 1981 to 2.8 m.t. in 1986. These increases, seen in table 6, took place despite the continuation of the Mexican eradication campaign.

Table 6. Mexican Opium Production and Participation in U.S. Supply, 1981-1986

	1981	1982	1983	1984	1985	1986
Production (m.t.)	16	17	17	21	28.4	20-40
% U.S. supply	36	34	33	32	39	41
Eradication (ha)	749*	1,185	2,500	3,700	3,190	2,380

*Includes only April to November 1981.
Source: NNICC *Reports*, 1983, 1984, 1985-1986.

---

[32] 1983 NNICC *Report*, p. 35.

The breakdown of the relative participation of the main sources of the U.S. heroin supply from 1981 to 1986, shown in table 7, indicates that the Mexican supply decreased from 36 percent in 1981 to 32 percent in 1984 but then increased in 1985 (39 percent) and 1986 (41 percent). Heroin consumption in the United States has been estimated at 6-7 m.t., and the number of addicts at around 490,000. This number, however, is still based on the 1981 survey.[33]

Table 7. Participation in the U.S. Heroin Market by Source, 1981-1986 (percentages)

	1981	1982	1983	1984	1985	1986
SW Asia	54	52	48	51	47	40
Mexico	36	34	33	32	39	41
SE Asia	10	14	19	17	14	19

Source: NNICC *Reports*, 1983, 1984, 1985-1986.

Reported increases in the Mexican supply appear to have taken place in the context of growing opium production worldwide over the last seven years (see table 8).

Table 8. NNICC Estimates of Worldwide Opium Production (m.t.), 1981-1986

	1981	1982	1983	1984	1985	1986
Mexico	16	17	17	21	28.4	20-40
Afghanistan	225	250-300	400-475	140-180	400-500	500-800
Iran	400-600	400-600	400-600	400-600	200-400	200-400
Pakistan	75-125	50-75	45-60	40-50	40-70	140-160
SW Asia total	700-950	700-975	845-1,235	580-830	640-970	840-1,360
Burma	550	600	600	740	490	700-1,100
Thailand	50	57	35	45	35	20-25
Laos	50	50	35	30	100	100-290
SE Asia total	650	707	670	815	625	820-1,415

Source: NNICC *Reports*, 1983, 1984, 1985-1986.

This table shows that every other source of supply, with the exception of Thailand and Iran, increased its opium production, in some cases substantially. Table 8 also reveals that Mexican production was the lowest of all the sources mentioned, except for Thailand in 1986. According to the NNICC and the INCSR,

---

[33]See the 1985-86 NNICC *Report*, p. 66.

however, most of the opium produced in Southwest Asia is consumed domestically or, after being processed into heroin, exported to India or Western Europe. Similarly, a large part of the production of Southeast Asia is consumed in the region. In the case of the Mexican supply, however, the NNICC argues that "nearly all of the opium produced in 1985 and 1986 was believed to have been converted to heroin."[34]

The estimated hundreds of tons of opium produced in Asia seem to beg further explanation. For example, if Southwest Asian production for 1986 (between 840 and 1,360 m.t.) were transformed to heroin, it would be enough to produce 84-136 m.t. of the drug. There are no data on how much of this production actually is converted to heroin, but it seems that these estimates in general are extremely high, perhaps even exaggerated.[35] On the other hand, they tend to lend support to the U.S. government claim that the worldwide production of opium production by far surpasses the actual demand for heroin.[36] In any case, the data show a similar pattern in the production of opium and heroin to that found in the case of marijuana: Every time a source is suppressed or significantly reduced without corresponding reductions in the demand, the resulting vacuum is filled by a new supplier in a relatively short period of time.

THE MEXICAN SUPPLY OF DANGEROUS DRUGS

The Mexican supply of dangerous drugs,[37] less significant than that of marijuana and heroin, has received little attention in the last ten years, though it was highlighted as a source of concern in some reports to the U.S. Congress in the early seventies.[38] In the last five years the NNICC has reported only that an unknown number of diazepam tablets, a depressant, had been smuggled from Mexico.

---

[34]Ibid., p. 83.

[35]For example, in the past the NNICC assumed that Iranian production was as much as twice the new estimate. Compare the NNICC's 1984 *Report* with its 1985-1986 *Report*.

[36]See United States Department of State, Bureau of International Narcotics Matters, *International Narcotics Control Strategy Report, 1987*, pp. 31-32.

[27]The term "dangerous drugs" is frequently used in the NNICC's reports in reference to a heterogeneous mix of chemically synthesized drugs like LSD, PCP, and tranquilizers, among others—*editor's note*.

[38]See Murphy and Steele, *The World Narcotics Problem*, p. 14.

The bulk of the supply of these types of drugs is produced within the United States, for an abuser population estimated in 1982 to include 2.8 million stimulant users, 1.5 million sedative users, 1.1 million users of tranquilizers, and 10 million hallucinogen users. It is estimated that these abusers consumed around 3.02 billion dosage units in that year. For 1984, the last estimate, the amount was calculated at 3.06 billion dosage units.[39]

ILLICIT DRUGS AND MONEY LAUNDERING

Through available reports and data on eradication, seizures, persons arrested, and forfeiture of assets in the United States and Mexico over the last few years, we can affirm that the Mexican drug supply is controlled by highly organized trafficking groups that operate in both countries. These groups control the bulk of cannabis and opium poppy cultivation, carried out in large part by poor peasants.[40] It should be noted that the direct growers receive only a minimal share in the benefits of this trade. These growers probably have been tempted to cultivate cannabis or opium poppy as a result of Mexico's economic crisis and the continuous currency devaluation, in addition to low prices for and traditional difficulties in commercializing agricultural products.[41]

Drug trafficking rings also control the conversion of opium to heroin, the processing of cannabis plants into smokable marijuana, and the export and distribution of both drugs to the United States.[42] The control and direction of all these activities require organization, support, and financial resources. The controllers of the Mexican supply thus fit perfectly the INCB assessment with regard to the worldwide production of illicit drugs:

> These illicit activities are financed and masterminded by criminal organizations with interna-

---

[39]See the 1983 NNICC *Report*, pp. 27-31.
[40]In the last few years, however, Mexican authorities have found several cultivation sites controlled by traffickers utilizing sophisticated agricultural techniques. The seizure of more than two thousand tons of marketable marijuana in Chihuahua in November 1984 falls in this category. For more on this problem, see Procuraduría General de la República, *Campaña contra el narcotráfico y la fármacodependencia. Balance de trabajo* (press conference with the attorney general, Dr. Sergio García Ramírez, México, D.F., 14 May 1985), pp. 6-10.
[41]See the 1983 NNICC *Report*, p. 46.
[42]See President's Commission on Organized Crime, *America's Habit*, pp. 107-110, 144-148.

tional links and with accomplices in the financial circles. In certain regions, drug trafficking is closely inter-connected with other major criminal activities.[43]

According to several U.S. government sources, the economic value of the illicit drug trade in the United States amounts to an annual minimum of $50-70 billion, up to a maximum of $110 billion.[44] Although much of this money does not go to the criminal groups that control the sale of the illicit drugs, because "so much of the final retail price of illegal drugs consists of the markups of retail dealers and low level wholesalers,"[45] it is clear that criminal organizations have amassed literally billions of dollars dealing in drugs. To illustrate the point, according to NNICC estimates the average wholesale price of a pound of marijuana in 1985 was between $300 and $600. If Mexican production of the drug for that year was calculated at 3,000 to 4,000 m.t., it had a potential market value of $2.3 to $4.6 billion. The retail value would have been several times higher, since retail prices were calculated at $50-100 per ounce for the same year.[46] How much of this estimated production was effectively exported and finally consumed, we do not know. But if we consider that the estimated participation of Mexican supply was 32 percent of the total supply (estimated at 7,350 m.t.) and that the average price per pound was $450, we conclude that the Mexican supply for that year could be worth as much as $2.33 billion at wholesale prices.[47]

The question that emerges then is, where does all this money go, along with the billions annually spent by the U.S. consumers and drug addicts? In its *Interim Report* on *The Cash Connection: Organized Crime, Financial Institutions and Money Laundering*, the President's Commission on Organized Crime offered the following findings:

> Some $5-15 billion of the $50-75 billion in illegal drug money earned in the United States [annually] probably moves into international financial channels each year:

---

[43]See the 1986 INCB *Report*, p. 4.
[44]See President's Commission on Organized Crime, *America's Habit*, p. 5.
[45]See Kleiman, "Data and Analysis Requirements," p. 14.
[46]See the 1985-1986 NNICC *Report*, pp. 6-17.
[47]Ibid.

— More than two-thirds of the $5-15 billion is moved on behalf of foreign traffickers bringing drugs to the United States, as well as Colombians and Mexicans involved in distributing cocaine and heroin in the United States. The remainder comes from funds earned by the U.S. drug dealers and distributors.

— About one-third of the illegal drug money moves overseas in the form of currency, and much of the remainder is wired abroad after being deposited in the U.S. banking system.

— More than two-thirds of the $5-15 billion probably passes through Colombia, or the off-shore banking centers of the Caribbean Basin, mainly Panama, the Bahamas, and the Cayman Islands.[48]

These estimates suggest that the largest percentage of drug money, between 80 and 90 percent, never leaves U.S. territory; only 10-20 percent ($5-15 billion) goes into international financial channels. The largest part of laundering operations are therefore made within the U.S. banking system or in investments in the U.S. economy. Apparently—there is no special mention of this—no significant amounts of money from the overall drug trade are injected into the Mexican economy. The laundering operations that take place outside the United States are set up in Caribbean offshore banking centers, or in countries with strict banking secrecy laws like Hong Kong and Switzerland.[49]

One of the main findings of the President's Commission was that drug trafficking accounts for almost 38 percent of all organized crime activity in the United States, and that the largest part of organized crime's income comes from drug-related activities.[50] Thus, according to a Wharton Econometric Forecasting Associates estimate, $27.5 billion of a total U.S. organized crime net illicit income in 1986 of $44 billion, more than 62 percent, came from drug

---

[48]See President's Commission on Organized Crime Interim Report to the President and the Attorney General, The Cash Connection: Organized Crime, Financial Institutions and Money Laundering (Washington, D.C.: U.S. Government Printing Office, 1985), p. 13.
[49]Ibid., pp. 13-17. See also, United States Senate, Committee on Governmental Affairs Permanent Subcommittee on Investigations, Crime and Secrecy: the Use of Offshore Banks and Companies (Washington, D.C.: U.S. Government Printing Office, 1985).
[50]See President's Commission on Organized Crime, America's Habit, p. 7.

trade. This study also shows the extensive involvement of organized crime in such legal businesses as construction, food and liquor distribution, clubs and hotels, and banking and real estate, thus identifying organized crime as one of the largest industries in the U.S. economy.[51]

In sum, then, despite the growing eradication efforts made by the Mexican government and the growing quantities of drugs seized or interdicted by both countries, the supply of drugs has continued over the last four years. Trafficking rings have probably been reduced in number, partially as a result of law enforcement activities, but the remaining groups have become more violent and powerful than ever before. The economic resources at their disposal have grown enormously, along with their capacity to spread violence and corruption. The drug trade represents a major challenge to the governments and, indeed, the societies of both Mexico and the United States. It threatens the social, economic, and political structures of both nations. Drug traffickers can represent a threat to national security and a real danger to the stability of entire regions.

This section's portrayal of the Mexican supply of illicit drugs, and its interaction with other sources, clearly indicates that no viable solution can be attempted unilaterally because supply and demand are mutually dependent aspects of the same problem. The interactions of the Mexican drug supply with U.S. demand and other sources of supply also show the relatively new complexity of the phenomenon: They are part of a global problem of worldwide magnitude. It is possible that a durable bilateral solution is no longer attainable if other sources of supply are not also suppressed at the same time that attempts are made to reduce U.S. demand and Mexican supply.

THE FUTURE: PERSPECTIVES ON THE MEXICAN
SUPPLY OF ILLICIT DRUGS

It is not easy to present meaningful perspectives for the future for a problem that is determined by so many variables as is the Mexican supply of illicit drugs. There are some factors which

---

[51]See Sima Fishman, Kathleen Rodenrys, and George Schink, "The Income of Organized Crime" (study prepared by Wharton Econometric Forecasting Associates), in President's Commission on Organized Crime, *The Impact of Organized Crime Today*, pp. 463-487. The data on net income can be found in table 8.

certainly will continue to be very important, like the relative success and reinforcement of the eradication campaign and law enforcement activities in Mexico, particularly the disruption of the main trafficking groups. Clearly, too, the United States will continue to play a fundamental role in some of these tasks, especially in its law enforcement activities against organized crime. However, as shown in preceding sections, there are some other, more structural factors that have and will continue to have deep influence over the conformation of the Mexican supply of illicit drugs. Essentially, these are the existence of a huge demand in the United States and the low income of many peasants in several areas of Mexico.

As long as there continues to be an enormous demand for marijuana and heroin in the United States, and a willingness to pay high prices for these drugs, there will be Mexican, Latin American, and Asian peasants tempted by traffickers to cultivate and produce these goods. Obviously, if these two structural causes remain there will always be trafficking groups willing to profit from this situation. This could be a never-ending story, with growing eradication and seizures on the one hand, and continuous production and distribution on the other.

The negative economic, social, and political effects in both countries, even in the security area, are also growing and may continue to deteriorate the bilateral relationship with additional negative effects in other important areas. Obviously, neither of the two neighbors wants this scenario. The bilateral agenda will grow over the next fifteen to twenty years, not diminish, and the necessity of maintaining a workable relationship is real. The drug problem totally contradicts this requirement, vitiating an adequate negotiating environment for many other very important issues.

How, then, to escape the mutually dependent factors conforming the supply of Mexican illicit drugs and, more specifically, what can the governments of Mexico and the United States do to control drug trafficking?

The perspective of the Mexican and other Latin American governments has been to insist in the mutually dependent character of the supply of illicit drugs and the demand to which it responds. Moreover, Mexico has insisted that no durable solutions can be achieved in the fight against illicit drug trafficking as long as the demand continues. Mexico has also insisted on the necessity of offering cultivation alternatives to the growers, thereby inducing them to desist from cultivating illicit drugs. From the Mexican perspective, only policies directed toward confronting the deep causes of the illicit trafficking could be effective in the control of the problem.[52]

Until very recently U.S. strategy to control drug trafficking has been directed at the supply side, with the exception of several laws adopted in the 1960s and the 1970s and aimed at controlling demand through prevention, education, and rehabilitation programs. These activities, however, have never received top priority. The first priority has been to suppress the supply through crop control in source countries and interdiction of traffic on its way to the United States. As the President's Commission on Organized Crime has said,

> The history of Federal drug policy ... demonstrates that approaches to reduce supply have been the preferred and dominant Federal response over the last 75 years. It is only relatively recently that the nature of the drug supply-demand dynamic has become widely understood, leading to an increased appreciation for and emphasis on programs to reduce demand.[53]

Even the existing conventions that guide international cooperation in this area, largely inspired by the United States, clearly reflect this approach.[54] However, besides the continuous frictions that this emphasis on supply has produced between the United States and Mexico and many other countries, it has been largely ineffective, as evidenced by growing production, trafficking, and consumption of illicit drugs. Experience proves the impossibility of suppressing drug trade problems if there are not important reductions in demand. Experience also shows that an individual source, as in the case of Mexico in the late seventies, can at least

---

[52]See, for example, *Declaración de la delegación de México en la Conferencia Internacional sobre Abuso y Tráfico Ilícito de Drogas* (México, D.F.: Procuraduría General de la República, 1987), pp. 3-5.

[53]See President's Commission on Organized Crime, *America's Habit*, p. 187.

[54]The most important conventions are: 1) The 1961 Convención Unica sobre Estupefacientes and its 1972 Protocol. The Convención Unica has been ratified by 113 nations, including Mexico and the United States. 2) The 1971 Convención sobre Sustancias Psicotrópicas. This Convención has been also been signed by both Mexico and the United States. The texts of these international conventions can be found in: United Nations, *Convención Unica sobre Estupefacientes, 1961*, (New York: U.N. Publication Sales No. S.77.XI.3, 1977); and, United Nations *Convención sobre Substancias Psicotrópicas, 1971* (New York: U.N. Publication Sales No. E.78.XI.3, 1977).

temporarily drastically reduce its supply to near elimination, but other sources will emerge to fill the supply vacuum and, eventually, the same source will reemerge.

Experience also demonstrates another negative effect that drug trade may produce. After a period, a country affected by drug production can become an important consumption center, as happened in Pakistan and Thailand. Apparently, this is not yet the case of Mexico, although some partial studies suggest that consumption of some drugs has increased in the last fifteen years and the future might be different.[55] On the other hand, developments in the drug trade over the last two decades also show that a huge demand tends to create its own supply, as in the case of growing domestic marijuana cultivation and cocaine production in the United States.[56]

Because of the negative effects that almost always follow drug trade, some experts have been suggesting since the 1920s that legalization of illicit drugs could be a better policy than trying to suppress them. According to this view legalization would remove the profits of illicit trafficking, and thus reduce drug-related crime. This suggestion has been made about marijuana in particular.[57] However, until now no government has moved in this direction, and it seems very unlikely that any will try to promote this view in the near future. On the contrary, recent developments indicate that there is a consensus that drug abuse constitutes a growing worldwide social problem that must be dealt with through policies directed at simultaneously reducing demand, trafficking, and supply. The international dimension of the drug trade has convinced many governments that unilateral policies are bound to fail and that a worldwide effort is urgently needed.

This new consensus was evident during the June 1987 United Nations International Conference on Illicit Trafficking and Drug Abuse in Vienna, Austria.[58] The position adopted by the Conference has two main elements:

---

[55]There are no general studies available on the prevalence of drug abuse in the Mexican population. Most indicators refer to the middle- and upper middle-school student populations. See also, Secretaría de Salud, Consejo Nacional contra la Fármacodependencia, Instituto Mexicana de Psiquiatría, *Programa contra la Fármacodependencia* (México, D.F.: Secretaría de Salud, 1985), especially pp. 14-31.

[56]On the problem of increased cultivation of marijuana and production of cocaine within the United States, see Joel Brinkley, "Drug Production in U.S. Is Reported at Record Levels," *New York Times*, 1 June 1986: A1.

[57]See President's Commission on Organized Crime, *America's Habit*, pp. 330-332.

[58]See the *Declaración* adopted by the International Conference on Drug Abuse and Illicit Trafficking, Vienna, Austria, 17-26 June 1987, U.N. document A/Conf.133/

- The struggle against illicit drug trafficking and abuse must be comprehensive in its nature. It must include new policies and measures directed at all the factors conforming the problem, including a) prevention and reduction of demand, b) control of supply, c) suppression of illicit trafficking, and d) treatment and rehabilitation.

- The struggle has to be truly international and worldwide in scope. If not, the achievements obtained in one area or country can be offset by new increases in production, trafficking, or consumption in other countries.

This new approach contains an important commitment: While there is a clear understanding that countries affected by illicit cultivation, production, and trafficking must continue their law enforcement attempts to control the supply and suppression of illicit trafficking, the international community as a whole has recognized for the first time that policies directed at prevention and reduction of demand and treatment and rehabilitation are equally essential to control the illicit drug trade.

The mutually dependent character of both approaches is also present in a new draft international convention explicitly designed to confront the problem of illicit trafficking. This draft convention, originally proposed by several Latin American countries, has received enthusiastic support from the U.S. government. While some of its provisions call for such new measures against traffickers as forfeiture of assets and equipment, improved extradition procedures, and controlled delivery techniques, it also contains a provision calling for new measures to encourage the gradual elimination of demand for illicit drugs, thus eliminating the financial incentives for illicit trafficking.[59] For the first time, states party to this convention would be legally obliged to adopt and pursue policies to reduce internal demand for illicit drugs, and at the same time implement policies directed at disrupting drug trafficking.

The conference also adopted, without objection, a Comprehensive Multi-disciplinary Outline of Future Activities Relevant to the Problem of Drug Abuse and Illicit Trafficking, containing

---

MC/L.1 (Part III). See also the *Plan amplio y multidisciplinario de actividades futuras para el control del abuso de drogas ilícitas,* adopted at the conference, U.N. document A/Conf.133/MC/L.1 (Part II).

[59]See the text of the convention in the *Convención de las Naciones Unidas contra el tráfico ilícito de estupefacientes y sustancias psicotrópicas,* U.N. document E/CONF/82/15. See especially the text of article 14, "Medidas para erradicar el cultivo ilícito de estupefacientes y eliminar la demada ilícita de drogas."

thirty-five target activities to be pursued by countries affected by cultivation, production, traffic, or consumption of illicit drugs, depending on their individual situations.[60] Some targets contained in the outline may be particularly relevant to the illicit drug trade between Mexico and the United States. These would be some additional activities or policies that could be reinforced in Mexico, others in the United States, and many in both countries.

Prevention and Reduction of Illicit Demand:

- Assessment of the extent of drug misuse and abuse.

- Prevention through education.

- Prevention of drug abuse in the workplace.

- Prevention programs by civic and community special-interest groups and law enforcement agencies.

- Evaluation of the role of the media.

Controlling Supply:

- Strengthening the control of international movements of psychotropic substances.

- Control of the commercial movement of precursors, specific chemicals, and equipment.

- Redevelopment of areas formally under illicit drug crop cultivation.

Suppressing Illicit Trafficking:

- Disruption of major trafficking networks.

- Increased use of the technique of controlled delivery.

- Facilitation of extradition.

---

[60]The declaration and the outline are not binding, as usual for this kind of document adopted at international conferences. Nevertheless, they reflect new norms that will guide international cooperation in this field in the future. The new convention is binding for the states that are party to it.

- Mutual judicial and legal assistance.

- Forfeiture of the instruments and proceeds of illicit drug trafficking.

Treatment and Rehabilitation:

- Progress toward a policy of treatment.

- Inventory of available modalities and techniques of treatment and rehabilitation.

- Training of personnel working with drug addicts.

- Social reintegration of persons who have undergone programs for treatment and rehabilitation.

These targets are very general, and most are currently pursued in both countries. Nevertheless, they underline some priorities and, above all, are the clearest recognition of the interdependent factors that order the struggle against drug trafficking and abuse. At this stage it is impossible to predict how successful the struggle could be if these goals are really pursued by both countries. But we can predict that the drug trade will maintain its present dimensions, perhaps even increase if these targets are not firmly and cooperatively pursued.

The question of bilateral cooperation leads to further comments on the political dimension of the drug problem. Historically, the issue of the drug trade has been an important topic in the internal political debate in the United States. It is one of those issues that can be a deciding factor in presidential and congressional election campaigns, as in the 1968 presidential race, when Richard Nixon was elected, and the 1986 congressional campaign. In both instances Mexico was harshly criticized or became the object of political pressures and decisions like the two Operation Intercept programs, whose real effectiveness for the stated purpose was, at best, highly dubious. As difficult as it is to separate the drug-trafficking problem from politics, given the very negative consequences that these attitudes may have in other areas and for the bilateral relation as a whole in the future, it would be desirable that at least the U.S. federal government resist the temptation to use the drug problem as an instrument of internal politics.

The government of Mexico has a major interest in controlling the activities of drug traffickers and in ensuring that they cannot operate as an independent power that could challenge the government for control of entire regions, spreading more violence and corruption. Therefore, and considering the enormous resources that the traffickers have at their disposal, it seems that a long and violent struggle between the government and trafficking groups is almost unavoidable. In this respect, law enforcement activities in the United States will be of fundamental importance. No doubt, U.S. organized crime has acquired vast economic resources from the drug trade. Moreover, it seems that these resources have become an important economic force in areas like Miami and New York. It is clear that trafficking groups would be substantially reduced in number and economic force if they were denied access to their assets.

A new approach to deal with the drug trade is being adopted by the international community. There are some signs that U.S. policy is also changing in that direction. Apparently, there is an increased social mobilization within the United States that may lead to decreases in the current high consumption levels over the medium term. At this stage it is impossible to assess whether this positive trend will be sustained long enough to reverse the growth trend of the drug trade.

Finally, there remains the other structural factor that shapes the Mexican supply of illicit drugs: the low incomes of Mexican growers. The removal of this factor will no doubt take time. It will require patience, imagination, and, above all, economic resources that the country lacks, particularly during the current economic crisis. Eradication programs will not suffice, even if they are followed up by the best law-enforcement practices. In the medium and long term, only redevelopment of those areas can offset the economic incentive to cultivate illicit drugs. In the final analysis, without redevelopment alternatives for the growers, international and bilateral efforts to control the illicit traffic are exercises in futility, "tantamount to trying to repeal the law of supply and demand, if not human nature itself."[61]

---

[61]See Robert W. Gregg, "The International Control System for Narcotic Drugs," in *Drugs, Politics and Diplomacy*, ed. R. Simmons and Abdul A. Said (Beverly Hills, Calif.: Sage Publications, 1974), p. 300.

II

POLICIES AND POLICY ALTERNATIVES

4

U.S. Narcotics Policy toward Mexico: Consequences for the Bilateral Relationship

Richard Craig

Illicit drug trafficking has emerged in recent years as both a national security issue and a foreign policy priority for the United States. Reinforcing a timeworn theme, the government's primary response to the problem has been to seek a solution at the foreign source, in those countries whose fields and laboratories produce the illicit products so demanded by American users. As a multi-ton producer of heroin and marijuana, and an increasingly important conduit for cocaine, Mexico has become a primary target of Washington's narcopolitics. This essay analyzes the multiple implications for the United States of its narcotics policy toward Mexico. It depicts such policy as cyclical, often unilateral, contentious, and incident prone. It begins with an historical review, analyzes the problem within a broader context of Washington's international narcotics control efforts, and treats the domestic and international repercussions for the United States of its policies toward Mexico.

HISTORICAL PERSPECTIVE

U.S. interest in illicit Mexican drugs can be traced to the onset of U.S. concern over its own drug abuse problems at the turn of the century. As is the case with Washington, international drug control efforts in Mexico date from the 1909 Shanghai Convention and the Hague Opium Convention of 1911-1912. As a signatory,

Mexico agreed to impose controls over licit opium to prevent its clandestine export. President Alvaro Obregón banned opium imports in the early 1920s. By 1931 Mexico had forbidden exports of marijuana and heroin and signed an international agreement calling for control of narcotic drugs at their source. More importantly for this analysis was the period 1936-40, during which American concern over burgeoning domestic abuse problems led Washington to encourage "the adoption by Mexico of a restrictive narcotic control policy similar to that of the United States."[1]

Such pressure was somewhat belated, however, since unofficial Mexican efforts against illicit opium cultivation began early in this century—when Chinese immigrants to Sinaloa and Sonora became the nation's first opium growers. In a strange historical about-face, the United States actually *encouraged* legal Mexican opium and hemp production during World War II on behalf of the Allied war effort. Unfortunately, cultivation of both products increased dramatically, and by 1943 opium had become Sinaloa's largest cash crop. During the same year, U.S. officials reversed their pro-production approach toward Mexican drugs, again encouraged restriction, and even discussed the possibility of border searches for drugs. Clandestine cultivation and trafficking increased following the war, despite the launching in 1948 of Mexico's initial nationwide antidrug campaign. In response, the United States protested to the Economic and Social Council what it deemed Mexican laxity in halting such activity. Mexico then vowed to increase its efforts, and Washington dropped its protest.[2] The pressure-response scenario of U.S.-Mexican narcopolitics had thus been well established by the late 1940s.

Equally manifest during the earlier years of Mexico's *campaña antidroga* were four facts which still hold true today. First, the remote and often inaccessible areas where marijuana and opium poppies are grown make the utilization of aircraft requisite to success. Second, without the extensive use of herbicides, a truly successful campaign against the cultivation of opium and marijuana is impossible. Third, any effort to control or eradicate the cultivation of and traffic in Mexican drugs is met with violence. Fourth, every new and accelerated government effort produces an

---

[1]See W.O. Walker, III, "Control across the Border: The United States, Mexico, and Narcotics Policy, 1936-1940," *Pacific Historical Review* 47 (1978):92.
[2]See W.O. Walker, III, "The International Politics of Drug Control," paper presented at the meeting of the Latin American Studies Association, Bloomington, Ind., October 1980.

innovative trafficker response, renewed production, and pressure from Washington.

During the 1950s Mexico's antidrug efforts were severely hampered by lack of aircraft, spare parts, and skilled pilots. All the while, Mexico's program came under increasingly critical scrutiny in congressional hearings. In January 1961 an interdepartmental report noted that virtually all illicit drugs on the American market originated in Mexico. It was not until late 1961, following an informal U.S.-Mexico meeting on the narcotics issue, that Mexico began to acquire from Washington the equipment it needed to conduct a more successful campaign.[3] The results were impressive, particularly the number of opium plots destroyed. In the interim, however, American demand grew exponentially.

Increasing amounts of Mexican marijuana and a consistent supply of heroin entered the United States during the 1960s, as an alienated youth culture became the "turned on" generation. Responding to mounting drug problems, the Nixon administration began new diplomatic initiatives designed to ease America's drug dilemma by attacking the problem at its foreign source. While Turkey became the primary target of Washington's heroin diplomacy, Mexico came under increasing diplomatic pressure as the principal supplier of marijuana.

Such pressure was epitomized by the launching on September 21, 1969, of Operation Intercept, "the nation's largest peacetime search and seizure operation by civil authorities." The unilateral offensive was designed ostensibly to halt the flow of marijuana into this country in one massive maneuver. In reality, it constituted a classic example of economic blackmail designed "to get the Mexicans to come around and really start doing something about dope." Perhaps, in the long run, Intercept did succeed in "bringing the Mexicans around." However, in the short run, it became a major diplomatic incident and was replaced on October 11 by Operation Cooperation, a face-saving binational arrangement, remnants of which are evident today.[4]

The relative merits and demerits of Operation Intercept will long be debated. There is no doubt, however, that it constitutes a

---

[3]See J.W. Van Wert, "Government of Mexico Herbicidal Opium Poppy Eradication Program: Summative Evaluation" (Ph.D. dissertation, University of Southern California, 1985).

[4]See R.B. Craig, "Operación Intercepción: una política de presión internacional," *Foro Internacional* 22 (1981):203-230.

benchmark in U.S.-Mexico narcotics diplomacy and a turning point in Mexico's antidrug campaign. Despite its negative impact, Intercept spawned several positive developments: Under its successor, Operation Cooperation, the binational antidrug effort between Mexico and the United States improved annually until 1985. Furthermore, the unilateral American action was in part responsible for a revived, expanded, and far more thorough Mexican campaign. And, as an indirect result of Intercept, Mexico came to admit publicly the existence of a growing domestic drug problem and to address the question as an integral part of its national campaign.[5]

As its share of the bargain under Operation Cooperation, Mexico accelerated manual eradication and interdiction efforts, particularly against the expanding cultivation of opium poppies in the "critical triangle" of Sinaloa, Durango, and Chihuahua. For with Turkey's agreement in the early 1970s to strictly control opium production, Mexico soon became the principal source of heroin on the U.S. market and, as a result, the primary object of Washington's ever more aggressive international narcopolitics. Stepped up eradication efforts by the military proved largely futile, however, due to problems of transportation, geography, and technology. At this juncture the Mexicans made the most critical decision in the history of their *campaña*: With U.S. assistance they would launch an unprecedented aerial herbicide program. Thus was born in the mid-1970s the phalanx of Mexico's contemporary antidrug program, Operation Condor.

Nothing before or since has so impacted the Mexican drug scene and so pleased the United States. Condor initially had it all:

- enthusiastic support of the Mexican Attorney General's Office, which administered the program and in the process acquired from the United States an air wing larger and better equipped than most Latin American air forces;

- a firm commitment from the secretary of defense—an army general and close friend of the attorney general—who saw in Condor an opportunity for his officers and men to gain valuable field experience in what often resembled antiguerrilla warfare;

- unprecedented coordination between Mexico's Federal Judicial Police, the military, and U.S. narcotics officials;

---

[5]Craig, "Operación Intercepción."

- sincere anticorruption efforts, particularly the constant rotation of military zone commanders before they succumbed to the lure of narcodollars; and

- the largest airborne herbicide program in history, which had the political advantage of being impersonal or antiseptic.

Plants, not people, were Condor's focal point. And it eradicated plants, field after field of poppy and marijuana, year after year.

Mexico became Washington's showcase of what determination and cooperation could achieve. And Condor also salvaged Mexico's international image. Representatives from Asia, the Middle East, and Latin America came to the Mexicans for advice on how best to attack the drug curse. Moreover, Condor proved the means by which Mexico City reclaimed control of the lawless *triángulo*. In effect, the Mexican army "depistolized" the countryside and in so doing killed two birds with one stone: drug cultivators/traffickers and real or imagined guerrillas. In the process it eliminated a direct challenge to the national government's legitimacy at regional and local levels. Third, the attorney general acquired a formidable air force.

Operation Condor's multiple impacts on the American drug scene were impressive. According to State Department sources, Mexican "brown" captured roughly 85 percent of the heroin market in 1974. Two years later the figure had slipped to 53 percent, and by 1980 it had dropped to 37 percent. Simultaneously, the average retail purity of Mexican heroin seized at the border decreased markedly from 70 percent in 1975 to 25 percent in early 1979. Finally, deaths resulting from heroin overdose declined 80 percent from 1976 to 1979. And what was true of heroin as a result of *la campaña* was even more evident in the case of marijuana, as the Mexican share of the U.S. market shrunk from an estimated 90 percent in 1974 to roughly 5 percent in 1981.

Given such results, what happened in the 1980s to tarnish the image of Mexico's antidrug program and in the process bring U.S.-Mexico narcopolitics, and U.S.-Mexican relations in general, to their lowest point since Operation Intercept? More pointedly, how do we explain the resurgence of Mexican drug traffic in the face of Operation Condor and the entire *campaña permanente*?

Unicausal explanations must be ruled out, for it was a combination of factors, including the weather, that marked the resurgence of Mexican drug trafficking. The year 1984, for example, marked a large increase in Mexican drug production. It was also unusually wet—it even rained in the dry season. This meant more bountiful crops, legal and illegal. It also meant lower ceilings, fewer clear days for aerial spraying, and less adhesion of herbicide to plant.

A less natural variable is grower/trafficker ingenuity. Poppy fields were made smaller and planted year round in new areas— under canopies, cliffs, and at heretofore unheard of altitudes of up to 9,000 feet. Mexico's narco air force contained no aircraft capable of flying and spraying at such heights, a deficiency that has now been remedied.

A third cause was bureaucratic ineptitude and mismanagement. The coordination which highlighted Condor's initial years deteriorated. It was replaced by bickering and interservice/interagency rivalries. As a result, some plots went unsprayed, some were sprayed too late, and others were sprayed two and three times. Much of this resulted from the lack of an independent verification system and an accurate aerial survey of growing zones. The verification problem appears to have been at least partially remedied by Operation Vanguard, the 1987 cooperative agreement which involves direct post-spraying aerial observations.

Fourth, Colombia's emergence as a major drug-producing center meant a greater and more profitable role for Mexican *traficantes* as cocaine transshippers. With Washington's Florida and Gulf Coast interdiction programs, smugglers shifted routes. More than one-third of the cocaine reaching the United States is believed to be routed through Mexico by way of the Yucatán Peninsula.

Economic deterioration also played a crucial role in revitalizing the Mexican connection. A government facing mounting economic pressures was less willing—and understandably so—to devote ever scarcer resources to antidrug measures. With this economic downslide has come greater desperation on the part of already desperate peasants. If they had little to lose years ago by raising marijuana, today's campesinos have absolutely nothing to lose. On the contrary, with the constantly rising value of the dollar vis-à-vis the peso, they and their trafficking *patrones* have very much to gain.

Corruption was certainly another very important element. The traffickers pay in dollars. In today's Mexican economy, the dollar talks louder than ever, especially in drug zones. Imagine, for example, the dilemma of one young drug zone supervisor in the northwest. It has been said with some authority that he refused a $1 million trafficker bribe in the fall of 1983.

The above incident indirectly represents another variable in the deterioration equation: demand from across the border. American demand for the three major illicit drugs has not decreased in the 1980s. It has remained essentially constant for heroin, decreased slightly for marijuana, and increased exponentially for cocaine. Inseparable from the pull factor of demand are, of course, profit—megaprofit—violence, and corruption.

Finally, and perhaps most importantly, there were the twin variables of inertia and complacency. On the Mexican side, programs tend to ossify during the final years of a *sexenio*. This problem, along with unprecedented corruption, reached acute levels under José López Portillo. The *campaña* suffered from neglect, lack of guidance, and a dearth of leadership enthusiasm during 1981 and 1982. And 1983 was a transition year for the new narco bureaucrats. In Washington, meanwhile, Mexico's program was taken essentially for granted. Condor was still destroying fields of dope from the air with herbicide. It was still the model to be emulated. Colombia was the problem of the 1980s.

In effect, the United States came to treat Mexico's *campaña* as another foreign aid program. Washington would furnish aircraft, technology, and instruction. Mexicans would furnish money, men, and a desire to master the arts of crop destruction and trafficker interdiction. Once they had done so, the United States would conduct a phased withdrawal, eventually leaving the entire show to the Mexicans. Both countries supported this game plan, and before the economic downturn Mexico even called for a more rapid end to the American role. But Mexico City and Washington neglected one key fact: the drug phenomenon does not fit classical development models, particularly during serious economic crises.

POLICY EXAMINED

The student of U.S. antidrug programs with Mexico encounters two fundamental questions. The first involves a broad question, one beyond Mexican narcotics: Does the United States in fact have an international drug policy? Answer: Yes, and it has displayed amazing continuity throughout most of this century. It consists of three core elements: crop eradication at the foreign source, hopefully through an aerial herbicide program; interdiction in the source nation or in route to the United States, preferably in cooperation with source state security forces; and elimination/ immobilization of major traffickers, again on a cooperative basis.

Does Washington also have a bona fide *narcopolítica* toward Mexico? Again, the answer is affirmative. Dating back at least to the 1930s, it, too, with the wartime exception noted above, has shown marked continuity in goal and strategy: Keep illicit Mexican drugs out of the United States through eradication, interdiction, and immobilization *in Mexico!* In sum, Washington has steered a constant, easily definable course in search of a cure for the nation's drug abuse problem. Only in recent years, and then out of admitted desperation, has it seriously considered Pogo's aphorism, "We have met the enemy, and he is us!"

Along with Colombia, Mexico is the linchpin of America's international narcopolitics. It can, within reason, be called one of the three authentic success stories resulting from that policy, along with Turkey and Colombia. Judging from the size of Washington's diplomatic narcotics section and its Drug Enforcement Agency (DEA) contingent, Mexico is demonstrably the most important country in the world to the State Department's Bureau of International Narcotics Matters (INM). It is, according to INM statistics, the largest single source nation for marijuana and heroin on the U.S. market and a conduit for more than one-third of the cocaine. Such realities notwithstanding, Washington's drug policy with Mexico and U.S.-Mexico narcotics relations have been cyclical in nature, often unilateral, incident-prone, and highly contentious. Illicit drug traffic has in fact been the most acrimonious issue between the two countries since the late 1960s. It is the flash point of U.S.-Mexican relations and shows no sign of losing its spark.

Cyclical Policy

In practice, Mexico-U.S. narcopolitics since the Nixon administration have been cyclical in nature. This ebb and flow has been determined without exception by the American drug scene and Washington's interpretation of Mexico's role in that scene. Put another way, the relationship's tone depends on Mexico's share of the U.S. illicit drug market, particularly its heroin and cocaine components. The larger Mexico's share, the greater Washington's pressure to eradicate. The greater the pressure, the more confrontational U.S.-Mexico narcopolitics and bilateral relations in general. Conversely, when market share indicators are favorable, so too are relations. It is important to note that this interrelationship has held constant for many years, despite changes in administrations.

In this respect, it is noteworthy that marijuana has not figured prominently in Washington's narco game plan with Mexico since G. Gordon Liddy's Operation Intercept. It has served only as a statistic and occasional lever point, but never as a key determinant of strategy. That role has been played traditionally by heroin and shared more recently by cocaine in transit from South America. Mexico, on the other hand, has long viewed marijuana as its most serious drug of abuse and a dangerous stepping stone. It has placed as much, if not more, emphasis on cannabis destruction as on destruction of opium poppies. Mexico's heroin abuse problem is minimal and confined primarily to its northern border. In this regard, Mexico is unique. It is the world's only major opium/heroin producer without a notable heroin addiction problem.

Unilateralism

U.S. narcotics policy toward Mexico contains several inherent contradictions, one of the most obvious and diplomatically precarious being the tendency toward unilateral decision-making within a bilateral, cooperative framework. As a rule, Washington has relied on a cooperative approach during the peaks of its narcopolitics with Mexico. Consultation and mutual decision-making are the rules in harmonious times. However, it is during the valleys of the relationship, those periods when Mexico's share of America's drug market increases and/or unfortunate personal incidents mar the relationship, that Washington abandons its binational cooperative stance and acts unilaterally without consulting or even warning Mexico. To put it more bluntly, in times of exasperation over Mexican inaction against drug cultivation and trafficking, American officials—all too often those not directly involved in the day-to-day antidrug program—shift to a go-it-alone-and-damn-the-torpedoes mode. While wholly consistent with the prerogatives of an independent nation and generally effective in the short term (the Mexicans generally come around), such unilateral actions do little in the long run to benefit either Washington's narcopolitics or U.S.-Mexico relations. Instead, they add another log to the fire of Mexican resentment.

Incident and Acrimony

A third important variable in the tenor of U.S.-Mexico narco relations is the personal incident or tragedy followed by an escalating war of words and deteriorating relations. It has involved the undiplomatic roughing up of a Mexican consul by U.S. Customs during the original Operation Intercept, the rape and murder of an American tourist by local *traficantes*, the kidnapping and smuggling into the United States of a known Mexican trafficker, the Bronson-like freeing of young Americans from a Mexican border prison, the defaming of Mexico's national flag by a San Diego newspaper, the torture of one DEA agent in Mexico, and most poignantly the torture and murder of another. In varying degrees, the results were similar in each of the above cases and in others too numerous to mention: deteriorating narcopolitics and diplomatic acrimony.

It is noteworthy, particularly from a policy viewpoint, how little is learned by both nations from incident after incident, year after year. Neither Washington nor Mexico individually, or the two in concert, has developed a personal incident crisis strategy, one designed to reduce the damage to narcopolitics and overall relations of such inevitable events. It is almost as if both sides await such events for their cathartic effect. Sequentially, the pattern is roughly as follows: worsening narco relations, unilateral American initiative and/or personal incident, charge-countercharge, tensions in general relations, escalating rhetoric from officials and media, mediation by cooler heads, binational conferences followed by words of praise for one side by the other, and improved cooperative efforts.

Highly illustrative of the cyclical, incident-prone, unilateral nature of U.S.-Mexico narcotics relations was the tragic saga of Enrique Camarena. The domestic and foreign policy implications of the Camarena affair continue to haunt relations between our countries. His assassination in 1985 set off a diplomatic clash, the results of which will be felt for years to come. The murder of an American DEA agent in Mexico and the failure of Mexican officials to treat it with the urgency deemed necessary in Washington caused Reagan administration spokesmen to react publicly with undisguised bitterness, anger, and threats that made front page news for weeks. What is little understood in the United States is how Mexico responded to the murder and, more importantly, to the American outbursts.

Administration disgust over the kidnapping and murder was made abundantly clear through diplomatic channels, press conferences, news talk shows, and media interviews. The message from Ambassador John Gavin, former DEA chief Francis Mullen, DEA agents in Mexico, and above all the media was blunt: The death of Camarena and his Mexican pilot, Alfredo Zavala, could have been avoided had Mexican officials heeded U.S. advice during prior months concerning the identities, whereabouts, and modus operandi of principal *traficantes*. The Mexicans had not arrested a major drug figure in many years. Guadalajara and other Mexican resort towns, compromised by drug capos, were too dangerous for American tourists. Most importantly, Mexico's antidrug campaign was said to be in shambles as the result primarily of blatant corruption from top to bottom.

Mexican reaction to the entire Camarena episode must be analyzed from two perspectives: how most individuals, private or public, responded to the event and its immediate aftermath, and how they reacted to Washington's response. Virtually all Mexicans were disgusted over the murders and what they implied for the country. Knowledgeable citizens realized that narcotics trafficking is a serious national dilemma, one that has cost the lives of several hundred soldiers and police over the last decade. But such bravado? They are also aware that the primary factor behind Mexico's drug dilemma is American demand. And as regards corruption and its gutting of the *campaña*, this phenomenon, in any form, was hardly shocking. Since becoming president, Miguel de la Madrid's second priority, after economic recovery, had been moral renovation, attacking the evils of corruption. It was not the reality of the drug program's corruptibility but the extent to which it had corroded the campaign that came as a surprise, particularly its penetration of upper echelons of the Federal Judicial Police.

However, what truly stunned the Mexicans and their governmental officials was the public nature of Washington's criticism. This in turn touched the hypersensitive nerve of Mexican nationalism and turned a serious, regrettable event into a vitriolic diplomatic incident. All the old ghosts were hauled out and paraded, particularly those of imperialism and American demand for drugs. Here we are, repeated the well-oiled Mexican press machine, fighting your war and sacrificing our lives to solve your drug problem. And you have the gall to attack publicly our sincere national effort because one foreign police agent operating in our country and his Mexican pilot were murdered by thugs. Is Camarena's death, regrettable as it may be—questioned the Mexicans—the true reason behind your official outburst? Or is it perhaps a pent-up response to our *dignidad*, our independent foreign policy, particularly in Central America? We simply must not, it was reasoned, permit one unfortunate event to spoil our otherwise amicable relations.

Washington's response was not long in coming: a personal call from President Reagan to President de la Madrid and meetings between secretaries of state and attorneys general. It was soon announced that Mexico would redouble its efforts, particularly against *narcocorrupción*. Washington would sing the praises of Mexico's effort in words and dollars. Both countries would return to fighting drug traffic and not one another. The Cortez incident of August 1986 notwithstanding, this is essentially what transpired. Mexico-U.S. narcotics relations were climbing out of the diplomatic depths, hopefully on their way to another peak.

POLICY IMPLICATIONS

While the results of illicit drug trafficking and abuse for American society, politics, and foreign policy are admittedly profound, we cannot yet establish any causal link between U.S. international narcotics policy and the nation's abuse problem. The same holds true of Washington's *narcopolítica* with Mexico. Critics abound, but no one knows what the results would be if the core precepts of one or the other were changed somewhat, altered fundamentally, or abandoned entirely. At this juncture we can only imply, not quantify.

Commitment

One of the first questions that arises from a study of U.S. narcotics policy with Mexico is that of commitment: Just how serious is America's determination to solve its drug abuse problem? More pointedly for comparative purposes, how determined is its effort vis-à-vis Mexico's? Granting the obvious flaws and problems in its program, Mexico's relative sacrifices in terms of spending, personnel, and lives lost in recent antidrug efforts exceed those of Washington, and this at a time of unprecedented economic crisis and political instability. To its credit, the Reagan administration budgeted more funds and assigned more personnel to its antidrug program than any of its predecessors. But considering the problem's scope, it still amounted to a small drop in a very large bucket.

Corruption/Violence

The twin curse of drug-related violence and corruption is evidenced throughout this nation. U.S. citizens are well aware of violence and corruption in Mexico, problems magnified by illicit drug trafficking. But they seldom take time to notice how seriously drugs have corrupted the United States at individual and institutional levels. Americans in all walks of life, from farmers to judges, have fallen prey to the lure of narcodollars. This is not to claim that U.S. narcopolitics has caused the problem; it may have been as bad or worse had the policy been different. It is simply to note the obvious: U.S. policy has failed to stem the tide of drug-related corruption and violence. The twin correlates of *narcotráfico* have reached unimagined heights in this country during recent years. And some of the worst manifestations are evidenced along the nation's southern borders.

Border Ambience

The multiple impacts of illicit drug trafficking are felt most acutely along the U.S. border area with Mexico, and they are even more pronounced if one extends the line to include southern Florida. The border has been described as "penetrable almost at will," "completely out of control," a "porous sieve," and a "smuggler's dream." Despite increased manpower, the latest in detection/ interdiction technology, and on-again, off-again, search-and-discourage operations, drug smuggling has increased alarmingly. With it have come turf battles among border law enforcement agencies and serious repercussions for border residents, including manifold increases in drug-related violence, corruption, and abuse.

Narcotics traffic, more than any other issue, has strained traditionally friendly transboundary relations. All the while, control of day-to-day affairs has slipped from the hands of those who manage them best—those who live on the border—into the hands of those who know the least about the area—federal bureaucrats.

The deleterious effects of drug trafficking have changed the ambience of many border cities during the 1980s. Washington's border interdiction policy has proven ineffective; it has been overwhelmed by the illicit drug wave. Meanwhile, some border residents and savings institutions have prospered from the drug business, and hopefully the U.S. Defense Department has learned just how vulnerable the nation's southern flank really is.

Perceptions

A fourth manifestation is more indirect and personal. It involves American perceptions of Mexico and its people, and it emanates from media coverage of the drug issues. The U.S. media, while at times granting Mexico's antidrug program its dues, tend to highlight the negative, the sensational. As a result, the American public, never one for in-depth knowledge of things Mexican beyond Fernando Valenzuela's ERA, has synthesized a new Mexican stereotype. The "Cisco Kid" and "Speedy Gonzalez" have been replaced by "El Negro," Caro Quintero, and "Don Neto." Not to be outdone, the Mexican press has itself created the new "average American" (a *drogadicto*) and a new list of "Gringo Bad Guys" headed by a former ambassador, an eloquent Customs chief, and the taciturn senator from North Carolina.

U.S.-Mexico *narcopolítica* has assuredly not resulted in improved relations at the personal level. On the contrary, the response of both nations to the narcotics question has proven highly detrimental to relations writ large and small.

Control/Coordination

U.S. narcotics policy with Mexico has always been plagued by quality control problems. While its international drug program did not differ fundamentally from those of its predecessors, the Reagan administration's effort appeared particularly uncoordinated during times of U.S.-Mexico narcocrisis. The Camarena affair again provides an exemplary case study.

In the tragedy's immediate wake, it appeared for a time that nearly everyone connected with the administration went out of his way to "out-bash" the Mexicans. The attorney general then came forth to present a more conciliatory line, only to be upstaged that very evening by the custom commissioner's blanket condemnation of all Mexican drug officials as corrupt to the core. All the while, we were left to wonder who was steering the government's narco ship. Were the "loose cannons" in Customs, DEA, and Congress really "loose," or had they been intentionally "loosed"? Was the 1985 version of Operation Intercept a coordinated, systemwide decision or a spur of the moment retaliation by one agency head? Who was responsible? What were the actual short-term and long-term policy goals? Has either or both been realized? One hopes that a crucial lesson has been learned: Someone must coordinate and be held responsible for Washington's *narcopolítica* with Mexico, someone well versed in crisis management.

Deteriorating Relations

With the exception of Operation Intercept in 1969, drug control was generally an asset to U.S.-Mexico relations until Enrique Camarena's murder. This incident and its aftermath made clear how much the overall relationship had deteriorated and how important the narcotics issue is to both countries. It serves as a microcosm of the relationship's delicate nature. And perhaps most fundamentally, it brings into question Mexico's relative importance to U.S. foreign policy and America's national interest.

Honest observers cannot deny the depths to which Mexico's antidrug campaign had fallen by the spring of 1985. Neither can they question the heinous nature of Camarena's murder. He was literally beaten and tortured to death. It was the nature of the response and what it implied that perplexes even the most neutral observers. The reply was indeed "Mexico-bashing." It came at the worst possible time for Mexico, for U.S.-Mexico narcopolitics, and for overall relations between the neighboring states. How badly did relations deteriorate as a result? Did they reach their lowest point in recent years? Yes. Their lowest level ever? No. In President de la Madrid's own words, "the lowest point occurred in 1847, when they seized half our territory."

Things have improved since de la Madrid's remarks. They could hardly have gotten worse. Cooler heads prevailed. Politically expedient Senate votes were overridden. The binational antidrug effort was "back on track." U.S.-Mexico relations were "back to normal." Yet one still puzzles over their accelerated deterioration in the mid-1980s. What is missing is an explanation of the extent, the depth, and the official nature of Washington's response, particularly in light of Mexico's obvious importance to U.S. national interests. Perhaps the reasons are rather self-evident.

The Reagan administration, like all of its contemporary predecessors, did not truly deem Mexican friendship all that important. If amicable relations could be achieved on Washington's own terms (not including numerous concessions to Mexican sensitivity), fine. If not, especially when push came to shove, that was fine too. Short-term goals invariably supersede more important long-term interests during such binational crises. It appears that Washington's response to Camarena's murder also stemmed from administration frustrations with "things Mexican."

Such reasoning is not meant to give credence to any ulterior motives theory. Washington's outburst was not meant to punish Mexico for its Central American policy. But it did spring from an accumulation of frustrations over Mexican stances on various issues. One such problem, but only one, was the deterioration of Mexico's eradication program in the face of continued American warnings.

From Washington's perspective, Mexican policy initiatives on everything from economics to tuna had become an irritant. In the meantime, the feeling was that the United States had gone out of its way to help Mexico through its economic crisis. Camarena's murder provided a flash point. It afforded particular administration spokesmen a legitimate outlet, an opportunity to vent their frustrations over "things Mexican." Had the tragedy not occurred, it may perhaps have been necessary to invent it.

POLICY OPTIONS

The overall results of Reagan's international control program were discouraging. Abuse statistics, despite some tentatively encouraging trends, are disappointing across the board. Of the three major drugs of abuse, none is in short supply. Mexico's role in America's drug scene, while admirably minor during the late 1970s, has again reached major status. As a result, critics and *curanderos* abound.

The most logical policy option involves balancing priorities between supply and demand. Washington must place far more emphasis on the problem's demand side. This need not mean neglecting the role of source countries, but it clearly requires far more funding, less rhetoric, and new ways of perceiving the abuse problem in the United States. The Mexicans, along with a crescendo of voices from other source countries, have long reminded Americans of the glaringly obvious: The supply exists only because the demand exists. A second politically feasible option, and one favored by many Mexicans and Americans, couples demand reduction efforts with stepped-up law enforcement in the United States. Its backers argue for a "get tough" approach to trafficker *and* abuser, including the marijuana smoker as well as the cocaine capo.

Ironically, I have yet to meet a Mexican law enforcement official who did not favor the Reagan administration's *in-country* law-and-order policies over those of previous governments. In effect, most Mexicans, public and private, want American officials to practice what they preach, to do unto their narcotics lawbreakers what they demand that the Mexicans do unto theirs. They reason that if Washington couples a concerted demand reduction program with accelerated law enforcement efforts against grower, trafficker, and abuser, America's drug problem will be substantially reduced. There would then be no reason for Washington's *política de batón* (big-stick diplomacy) when it comes to America's drug abuse problem.

As regards the two policy options, several caveats are in order. First, there can be no doubt regarding the demand side of the question. Border law enforcement officers themselves are very pessimistic about the interdiction component. They have told me bluntly that personnel, equipment, and technology notwithstanding, demand must be reduced. For as long as the profit incentive remains so great, illicit drugs will continue to traverse the frontier. Second, the suggestion of coupling demand reduction with stepped-up law enforcement is perhaps logical. But it is also fraught with dangers, particularly for Mexico.

In the real world of U.S. narcopolitics, such a policy would admittedly amount to greater emphasis on demand reduction and domestic law enforcement. But it would also mean at least as much, and probably more, emphasis on the source country components (eradication/interdiction/immobilization) and far greater interdiction efforts along the border. We have already witnessed the first stage of such a strategy in Operation Alliance and in modifications of the *posse comitatus* statute allowing greater use of military resources in interdiction efforts. What we have yet to witness, however, is the ultimate extension of such a policy, the virtual militarization of the border. Given the realities of civil liberties, criminal procedure, and Gramm-Rudman, it is likely that "get tough" legislation in the United States will mean "get tough" with border traffickers, not more arrests of small-scale marijuana cultivators and smokers. American court dockets, jails, and prisons are already overflowing.

What this discussion of the demand and law-enforcement components of U.S. policy suggests is a modification (in the case of a bona fide demand reduction component, a major change) of extant programs. At this juncture, no other approach is politically or psychologically feasible. Neither the American public nor its politicians, let alone U.S. narcotics officials, would seriously consider any of the more radical approaches. Suggestions that the United States abandon its current strategy and opt instead for either legalization, the British system of heroin maintenance, or some combination thereof are fertile grounds for debate, but they stand no chance of receiving serious consideration in the foreseeable future. The only realistic option at this juncture involves the demand component. The priority of reducing demand must be upgraded to equal, if not superior, status with law enforcement and eradication. The American public, if not the administration, will support such a policy with its tax dollars.

Assuming that the current U.S. policy remains essentially intact, what additional options are available for its improvement, particularly as regards the Mexican components? The first suggestion involves a subtle yet crucial change in tenor. The program's rhetoric must be toned down; the major "drug warriors" must become verbal "peaceniks." Its spokesmen must cease to sensationalize. Do not tell us the drug war has been won when we have not begun to fight. Do not announce that we "have turned the corner" when we are still in search of the street. And please spare us the constant statistical docudrama in defense of particular departments and agencies. Who, for example, really believes that only some 10 percent of the marijuana on the U.S. market is home grown? American officials are so good (bad?) at this art that the Mexicans made the horrible mistake of repeating their error. If one totals all the Mexican campaign statistics that appear in news releases, the

Mexicans have destroyed more marijuana and opium in recent years than have ever been used by mankind in its entire history. Narco rhetoric, like statistics, has a way of escalating out of control at the worst times for U.S.-Mexico relations.

An equal reduction should take place in stated goals and expectations. This holds true for both countries. American narcotics officials should set realistic goals and standards for their own programs and for Mexico's. In this regard, it is crucial that Americans realize they are dealing with Mexico and Mexicans as they are, not as we would like them to be. In my mind, no American should ever be given responsibility for working with Mexican drug officials until knowing the true meaning of the term *"ahorita"* (literally "right now," but in practice, "sooner or later"). The same thing might well be said of Mexican officials when it comes to such expressions as free press and separation of powers.

Serious attention must be given to the near and distant futures of the drug phenomenon. Americans must plan ahead, devising strategies for a changing drug scenario. The U.S. scene has always been marked by fluctuations and new problems. Today the major issue is cocaine and its derivatives. Ten years ago cocaine was a problem on the horizon—crack was unheard of. Marijuana used to be deemed a soft drug; now it's called "two toke dope." Heroin maintenance was once a feasible alternative; the British experience and "black tar" render it unworthy of emulation.

Mexico's drug scene too is ever-changing. Drug abuse was once a problem for poor campesinos and *pelados*. Today, it also threatens the middle class, the elite, and their children. Ten years ago virtually no cocaine was smuggled through the country; today tons are seized annually. If, through some miracle, American demand declined appreciably, what would become of the in-country surplus? The real life tragedies of Colombia, Peru, Bolivia, and Pakistan are instructive. In the long run, Mexico will act to defend its interests and those of its people when it feels threatened, not when Washington demands it. This has been the case with illicit drugs, official American opinion to the contrary notwithstanding. (Many U.S. officials still cling to the notion that Mexico moves decisively against narcotics only in response to American pressure.) But in today's rapidly changing world of international drug trafficking, Mexico must be prepared to confront several possible threats, not only the one emanating by indirection from the north.

From a national interest perspective, the United States must place the issues of illicit Mexican drugs and U.S.-Mexico narcopolitics where they belong. First, Washington should assess the relative importance of Mexico in that national interest equation. If it is decided that Mexico is crucial to American interests, in deed as well as in word, and that drugs play an important part in that relationship, the United States should seriously consider the following policy initiatives.

First, it must thoroughly and impassionately evaluate the current and near future of America's drug abuse scenario. Second, it must move with utmost speed to address decisively the root of the problem, domestic demand. Third, it should seek a more stable, less confrontational, less acrimonious narcopolitical relationship with Mexico. And Mexico must reciprocate. This may be accomplished without fundamentally altering Washington's international narcotics control strategy. The key concepts need not be changed, but equal status *in fact* must be given to reducing demand. Eradication in Mexico is just as important to Mexico as it is to the United States. The verification system under Operation Vanguard, if it continues to improve on its record, could well eliminate most of the friction in this area. It is virtually impossible to corrupt highly accurate aerial surveys.

As part of a more harmonious atmosphere, Washington must seek to end its unilateral policy tendencies, in particular the on-again, off-again Operation Intercept syndrome. Mechanisms exist for consultation on such matters. And Mexico should be consulted. If it refuses to cooperate, that is Mexico's prerogative. It is during such talks that Washington may, if it chooses, demand greater cooperation on a particular issue. In such scenarios, each side knows where the other stands. There are no surprise actions.

Although it seldom affects binational relations directly, the Mexican military's role in the antidrug program is important and highly publicized in Mexico. Yet it is virtually ignored by Washington. Mexico has consistently assigned some twenty-five thousand army troops as well as naval and marine units to the campaign against illicit drugs. Many soldiers and sailors have lost their lives in drug-related assignments. The U.S. military attaché is keenly aware of the army's role in the program. But Washington, in its fixation with the airborne eradication initiative, pays scant attention to it. Military eradication figures, their accuracy notwithstanding, are not even included in official American statistics on

Mexico's illicit crop destruction. The army is a crucial actor in contemporary Mexico. Its role in the *campaña* merits closer attention in Washington.

A final suggestion involves the human rights variable in American support of Mexico's antidrug initiative.[6] Washington should monitor more closely its role, however indirect, in three areas of the *campaña*: herbicides, military atrocities in rural drug zones, and torture of accused drug violators. As regards herbicides, the pillar of Mexico's program, the jury is still out on their long-term ramifications for folk and fauna. The fact that Mexico manufactures these chemicals itself or purchases them elsewhere makes the decision wholly Mexican. But so long as Washington is the driving force behind the airborne effort, it is vulnerable to charges of guilt by association. A rather bizarre development in Colombia illustrates the potential problem. An American firm, on the verge of operationalizing a herbicide for coca, recently refused to complete the project for fear of injury to its own workers in the field and future Agent Orange-type class suits by Colombians. The project remains in limbo despite Colombian government protestations—they want to use the spray—and fulfillment of environmental impact requirements.

In the case of military "cleansing" operations in the countryside, the charge, particularly from leftists, of guilt by association is commonplace. The army is really not routing *traficantes*; it is depistolizing the campo, ridding it of antigovernment elements. This "rape of the campesino" is, of course, another result of American pressure. Charges of guilt by association also surround the torture of those arrested for drug violations. The Mansfield Amendment still forbids DEA presence during such interrogations, but the latent problem of American complicity remains. One of the most controversial human rights problems was effectively removed in the late 1970s with ratification of the prisoner transfer agreement, an idea originally suggested by Mexico's attorney general.

In conclusion, it seems but a truism to reiterate the importance of Mexico to U.S. national interests. My charge in this paper has been to analyze the implications of U.S. narcotics policy toward Mexico for American society and U.S.-Mexico relations. That most of my recommendations are addressed to Washington policymakers

---

[6]R.D. Craig, "Human Rights and Mexico's Antidrug Campaign," *Social Science Quarterly* 60 (1980):691-701.

in no way implies that I deem Mexico's antidrug program fault free.[7] By early 1985, the Mexican eradication and interdiction programs were in shambles. Washington was correct to criticize Mexico at that juncture, just as it had every right to react with righteous indignation over Enrique Camarena's assassination. In my opinion, resolution of the Camarena case would go far toward mollifying U.S. critics of the Mexican campaign. It is still the most important psychological barrier to more harmonious U.S.-Mexican narcopolitics.

---

[7]In this regard see R.B. Craig, "*La Campaña Permanente*: Mexico's Antidrug Campaign," *Journal of Inter-American Studies and World Affairs* 20 (1978):107-131; Craig, "Human Rights and Mexico's Antidrug Campaign"; and Craig, "Operation Condor: Mexico's Antidrug Campaign Enters a New Era," *Journal of Inter-American Studies and World Affairs* 22 (1980):345-363.

5

Controlling the U.S.-Mexican Drug Market

Samuel I. del Villar

The goal of this paper is to determine, first, the dimensions of the drug market affecting Mexico and, second, how the government can respond to it within the country's legal framework. It will also provide a basis for evaluating the costs and benefits of the various options available to the Mexican government for addressing the evolution of the drug market.

The paper is divided into two sections. The first analyzes the drug market in Mexico from a law-enforcement perspective. It examines the national market, the U.S.-Mexican market, and the impact which the generation of added value has on both. The second part of the paper considers the government's political, legal, and administrative responses to this illegal market. Among these are limited tolerance and increased coercion, two potential strategic options for controlling and reducing the scope of the drug market.

The moral, social, political, and cultural problems associated with drugs are often dealt with singly. Drug abuse or, more euphemistically, "drug dependency" is taken to reflect consumption or demand.[1] "Drug traffic" is used to refer to production,

---

[1]Secretaría de Salud, Consejo Nacional contra la Fármacodependencia, Instituto Mexicano de Psiquiatría, *Programa contra la Fármacodependencia*.

transportation, and marketing—that is, supply.[2] In fact, the drug market is a unified phenomenon—a market that comprises both demand and supply. Failing to view the drug market as an integrated market hinders both understanding and effective governmental responses.

MEXICO'S DRUG MARKETS

There are two important drug markets for Mexico. One is the domestic market, the integration of drug supply and demand within Mexico. The other is the international market, where Mexico plays a role in some or all phases of the supply process: production, transportation, and marketing. To a great extent, this market is created by demand in the United States.

The Domestic Market

Mexico has serious internal drug problems, reflected in survey results from 1976 and 1981 on nationwide use of drugs by middle- and upper-level students. These data served as the basis for the Ministry of Health's Program against Drug Dependency,[3] which reached the following conclusions.

- The national drug market affects all of Mexico. The survey grouped the states and the Federal District into thirteen regions, and found that drugs were in demand in every one. The most popular drugs were marijuana (in 1981 4.95 percent of the students had used it), inhalants (4.7 percent), tranquilizers (5.4 percent), amphetamines (4.31 percent), and cocaine (1.15 percent).[4] Health sector statistics confirm these use patterns. In 1983, 10,017 patients were treated for drug use in "specialized treatment centers" located in five of the regions surveyed.[5] A 1981

---

[2]Procuraduría General de la República, *Campaña de México contra el Narcotráfico* (México: P.G.R., 1986).
[3]Secretaría de Salud, *Programa contra la Fármacodependencia.*
[4]Unfortunately, there was a discontinuity in surveys. The 1976 survey "reported indices in 13 regions," and the 1981 survey examined 15 cities distributed in eight of these regions. Nevertheless, although the averages mentioned for 1981 exclude five of these thirteen regions, this does not alter the validity of the conclusion, since the thirteen regions showed use of those drugs for 1976. Procuraduría General de la República, *Campaña,* pp. 18, 26-30.
[5]Northwest region, 1,578 patients; northeast region, 1,279; central zone, 3,005; southern region, 395; Federal District and metropolitan area, 3,760. For percentage distribution by type of drug see Procuraduría General de la República, *Campaña,* p. 24.

survey conducted in fifteen state reformatories in nine of the thirteen regions indicates that 25 percent of the 8,431 patients questioned had consumed some type of drug.[6]

- By the late 1960s and early '70s, drug use in Mexico, as in other countries, was no longer restricted to minority groups but had extended into other sectors of the population, and drug abuse by the young was an undeniable problem.[7] In the five years between the two national student surveys, results indicate that the use of all substances had increased among student populations. This is particularly significant since the student population represents only about 30 percent of the fourteen-to-eighteen-year-old age group, and evidence indicates that drug use is even more widespread among young non-students.[8]

- Mexico's regions are differentially affected by the U.S. drug market. The surveys indicate that drug abuse in Mexico is highest in regions with closer ties to the U.S. drug market. In the 1976 student survey, marijuana consumption was greatest in Mexican regions (the northwest and the Gulf coast) which supplied the most important U.S. markets of the time. The greatest increase in marijuana consumption in Mexico between 1976 and 1981 occurred in the northwestern region (users jumped from 2.5 to 7.2 percent of the student population).[9] The surveys also correlate the highest rate of regional increase in marijuana consumption (from 1.4 to 9.7 percent of students surveyed) and cocaine (from 0.3 to 2.7 percent) with the emergence of Jalisco over Sinaloa as the important supplier of drugs to the U.S. market during the seventies and eighties. The Chihuahua-Coahuila border region and the Jalisco-Nayarit-Aguascalientes region register the highest increases in cocaine consumption between 1976 and 1981, from 0.2 to 1.6 percent and from 0.3 to 2.7 percent of the population, respectively. The survey of reformatories only found heroin users (6.8 percent of the inmates) in the prisons of the northwest (Tijuana, Hermosillo, Nogales, Culiacán, Mazatlán, and La Paz). Cocaine users were found in prisons in

---

[6]The survey did not consider regions 3 (Nuevo León and Tamaulipas), 4 (Durango, Zacatecas, and San Luis Potosí), 7 (Querétaro and Hidalgo), and 13 (Oaxaca and Chiapas). The percentage weight of each drug in regional consumption is included here.

[7]Procuraduría General de la República, *Campaña*, p. 14.

[8]Secretaría de Salud, *Programa contra la Fármacodependencia*, p. 20.

[9]Unfortunately, the student survey of 1981 did not cover Veracruz which, along with Tamaulipas, is one of the two key states supplying Mexican marijuana to the drug market in the eastern United States.

Ciudad Juárez, Piedras Negras, and Chihuahua,[10] that is, in the U.S.-Mexico border region.

• Highly toxic imported "hard" drugs, scarce and expensive in Mexico, are of marginal importance. Marijuana is the most popular drug among the student[11] and inmate populations.[12] Nevertheless, statistics from the toxicology program of the Department of the Federal District's Office of Medical Services indicate some cases of marijuana intoxication (0.27 percent of cases treated).[13] Psychotropic drugs, although highly toxic, can be obtained legally. Relatively abundant and inexpensive, they are easy substitutes for the scarcer and more costly marijuana, which surely accounts for their widespread use. The surveys show that there is no consumption of the "hard" drug, heroin, and the "soft" drug, cocaine, has the lowest consumption rate of all.[14] Consumption of these drugs is limited to border area prisons, as noted above. To date, there is no information on consumption of distilled, inhalable cocaine ("crack") in Mexico.

• There is no massive demand for drugs in Mexico, making for a poor drug market that is relatively unattractive to organized crime despite an increase in consumption and related social symptoms in recent years. It appears unlikely that an illegal market with attractive profit margins for large-scale organized crime will develop in Mexico.

Drug use remains very limited in Mexican society, although it has increased and may continue to do so. Demand for drugs is limited to small sectors of the population, although the deleterious impacts of drug use are felt throughout their communities. The

---

[10]Secretaría de Salud, *Programa contra la Fármacodependencia*, pp. 16, 25.

[11]The dichotomy of the greater incidence of marijuana use among the student population relative to the higher regional average for tranquilizers is due to the impact of use in the Federal District and in the metropolitan area of Mexico City, which represented 50 percent of the surveyed population and where the level of marijuana use was 4.1 percent, as compared with 3.7 percent for tranquilizer use. Secretaría de Salud, *Programa*, pp. 26, 28.

[12]The survey concludes that "25 percent of the 8,431 inmates studied in fifteen state prisons in the Republic reported having consumed drugs. The most used drugs were also marijuana, 12 percent; tranquilizers, 4.6 percent; and inhalants, 2.8 percent." Secretaría de Salud, *Programa*, p. 16.

[13]Cocaine and mescaline registered the same index as marijuana, 0.27 percent, against 3.24 percent for plastic solutions and thinner, and 1.62 percent for barbiturates. Secretaría de Salud, *Programa*, p. 16.

[14]An average regional level of 1.15 percent. Even in the Federal District and the metropolitan area of Mexico City, the rate of cocaine use was notably low—0.7 percent. What elevated the regional mean was the relatively much higher level of use in and around Guadalajara (2.7 percent), the northern regions (1.6 percent), and the northwest (1 percent). Secretaría de Salud, *Programa*, p. 30.

data reflect an enormous gap between rates of consumption in Mexico and United States. There is no reason to think that this gap will close in the foreseeable future.

Consumption of the expensive drugs—heroin and, increasingly, cocaine—which return huge revenues to organized crime remains extremely restricted. In contrast to Asian poppy-producing countries, Mexico finds heroin use foreign and repulsive to the national culture. Opium-poppy production in Mexico responds to U.S. demand, both legal (morphine) and illegal.[15] Coca trees do not grow in Mexico, and there is no tradition of chewing coca leaves as exists in Peru. Even marijuana, a more traditional product in Mexico and commonly found throughout the country, has a very marginal effect on Mexican social customs. The student surveys indicate that cocaine is still limited to a few members of the elite, who have consumption patterns very different than those of the average Mexican. The high cost of these drugs (always in dollars), the constant devaluation of the peso, and the drastic contraction of Mexicans' real income prevent the development of a significant market for these drugs in Mexico. Furthermore, these circumstances should reduce the national market for these drugs in future, leaving only isolated markets linked to tourist centers for foreigners.[16]

Many drugs are legally available in Mexico. This helps keep crime interests, organized crime in particular, at the fringes of the market. Inhalants, tranquilizers, and amphetamines can be obtained in any number of hardware and drug stores and hospitals, albeit under regulated conditions. Moreover, the institutional supply of some marijuana substitutes is a most effective factor in controlling prices and keeping organized crime out of the market, simply because it is not a profitable area of business. Interestingly, the increase in use of inhalants noted in the student surveys of 1976 and 1981 was significantly higher than the increase in marijuana use.[17] But in the areas most well known for international drug traffic

[15]James Van Wert, "El control de los narcóticos en México. Una década de institucionalización y un asunto diplomático," in México-Estados Unidos 1985, comp. Gabriel Székely (Mexico: El Colegio de México, 1986); Ethan Nadelman, "Cops Across Borders: Transnational Crime and International Law Enforcement" (Ph.D. dissertation, Harvard University, 1987).
[16]The increase in cocaine use registered in the 1976 and 1981 surveys of student population corresponded exactly to the period of the oil boom after the recession of mid-1986.
[17]While the regional average of use by mid- and upper-level students between 1976 and 1985 was 1.6 to 4.95 percent for marijuana, it was 1.03 to 4.75 percent for inhalants. The contrast for the Federal District and the metropolitan area of Mexico City was greater: 1.9 to 4.1 percent for marijuana and 1.6 to 4.6 percent for inhalants. Secretaría de Salud, Programa, pp. 22, 27.

(the northwest and the Guadalajara area), where marijuana is assumed to be abundant, marijuana use rose more quickly than use of inhalants.[18]

The national drug market is a priority for governmental health and social rehabilitation policies. However, the institutional market of easily produced industrial and pharmaceutical products that coexist with illegal drugs is not a primary objective of Mexican criminal legislation. Attempts to eliminate the institutional market would only lead to the development of a large black market in these products, the profits from which surely would finance organized crime. In this case, the "remedy" would be more harmful than the illness itself.

At present, and over the foreseeable future, Mexico's major problem with the illegal drug market exists beyond its borders, in the massive demand for marijuana, cocaine, and heroin in the United States.

The International and U.S. Drug Markets

Mexico plays a triple role in the international drug market, as importer, exporter, and importer-exporter. Mexico's significance as an importer appears to be marginal. Mexico imports a minimal amount of South American cocaine and raw materials and processed products required to satisfy the national demand for psychotropic drugs.

Mexico's illegal drug nightmare stems from its role as an exporter of marijuana and heroin and an importer-exporter of cocaine, demanded on a massive scale by the most powerful economy in the world. This drug flow responds to increasing drug addiction in the United States and the massive quantities of drug dollars to be had.[19]

---

[18]In the northwest, marijuana use among mid- and upper-level education levels of students rose from 2.5 to 4.2 percent between 1976 and 1981, while use of inhalants rose from 1.0 to 2.5 percent; in Guadalajara's zone of influence the variations were 1.4 to 9.7 percent for marijuana and 1.4 to 5.6 percent for inhalants. In the region comprising Tabasco, Campeche, Yucatán, and Quintana Roo, which is important for drug production and traffic through the northwest (Veracruz was not surveyed in 1982), the level of marijuana use increased from 0.7 to 5.0 percent and that of inhalants from 1.0 to 3.3 percent.

[19]Samuel I. del Villar, "La narcotización de la cultura en Estados Unidos y su impacto en México," in *México-Estados Unidos 1985*, comp. Gabriel Székely (Mexico: El

Estimates of the overall dimensions of the U.S. drug market, in terms of users and revenue, are imprecise and vary widely depending on who prepares them and for what purpose. Mark Kleiman presents the following figures on the number of users by drug type that form the U.S. market base.[20]

- 500,000 daily users of heroin, 1.5 million heroin users total;

- 500,000 habitual users of cocaine, five million monthly users, and ten million users total;

- 500,000 users of crack (inhalable, distilled cocaine);

- 3 million marijuana users who consume the drug more than once a day and 20 million who use it regularly;

- 200,000 users of PCP; and

- 2.5 million people who illegally use hallucinogens, barbiturates, amphetamines, synthetic compounds, and tranquilizers.

The U.S. market for illegal drugs thus comprises some 37.7 million regular drug users. The number could be more than twice that if irregular drug users are counted, reaching 75-80 million or more regular and irregular users on the demand side of the drug market. Even allowing for the double counting that could occur in these estimates because of individuals who use several different drugs, estimates indicate that there is an aggregate market of nearly 100 million users.

The extraordinary breadth of this market is corroborated by surveys conducted by the National Institute on Drug Abuse of the U.S. Department of Health and Human Services. Its last two national surveys—conducted in 1982[21] and 1985[22]—provide information on drug abuse among the young and young adult U.S. population and offer additional bases for calculating the total dimensions of the U.S. illegal drug market.

Colegio de México, 1985). For a broader view, see *The Illicit Drug Market between Mexico and the United States* (New York: Council on Foreign Relations, in press).

[20]A.R. Mark Kleiman, "State and Social Drug Law Enforcement, Issues and Practices," mimeo. (Cambridge, Mass.: Program in Criminal Justice Policy and Management, John F. Kennedy School of Government, Harvard University, March 1987).

[21]National Institute on Drug Abuse, *National Survey on Drug Abuse: 1982* (Washington, D.C.: U.S. Government Printing Office, 1983).

[22]National Institute on Drug Abuse, *Drug Use among American High School Students, College Students, and Other Young Adults. National Trends through 1985* (Washington, D.C.: U.S. Government Printing Office, 1986).

The report on the results of the 1982 survey noted that:

> For today's young people, trying marijuana is, apparently, a part of normal maturing pattern. But the experience of having used marijuana is not only generalized among the young 12 to 17 year olds and among young adults of 18 to 25 years, but it is increasingly common among the group from 26 years and up....
>
> While 27% of all young people have tried marijuana, the rate of lifetime prevalence varies from 8% for the 23 and 13 year olds to 24% for the 14 and 15 year olds and 46% for the 16 and 17 year olds. The rate of lifetime prevalence reaches its highest level during the years of young adulthood, with 64% of the group of 18 to 25 year olds reporting that they have at least tried marijuana.
>
> Because the opportunities to use marijuana were not generalized until the end of the 1960s and 1970s, the majority of persons now in their 40s or 50s or older were not exposed to marijuana during the "high risk" years of adolescence. Thus, the rates of life prevalence in 1982 calculated separately for different age groups of adults indicate that the 64% "peak" of young adults gradually diminishes ... to 60% for persons of 26 to 29 years, 53% for those of 30 to 39 years, and 24% for 35 to 40 year old adults ... and to only 5% for persons 50 years old or over.... Nevertheless, among older adults, now parents of children from 12 to 17 years of age, one out of every five reports having at least tried marijuana sometime in his or her life. Apparently, what at one time was known as the marijuana generation gap now is a thing of the past for many U.S. families.[23]

---

[23]Of the 27 percent of young people (12 to 17 years) who used marijuana, 5 percent did so over 100 times and 13 percent between three and ninety-nine times. Of the 64 percent of young adults who are users, 24 percent used it over 100 times, 30 percent between three and ninety-nine times and 10 percent between one and two times. National Institute on Drug Abuse, *National Survey*, pp. 1-30. The cited quotation is translated from a Spanish version of the original—*editor's note.*

Regarding the use of other drugs, the survey concluded that:

- 10 percent of young people 12 to 17 years, 28 percent of young adults (18-25 years old), and 9 percent of older adults (26 years old and up) had used psychotropic drugs for nonmedicinal purposes.

- 6 percent of young people, 28 percent of young adults, and 9 percent of older adults had used cocaine.

- 5 percent of young people, 21 percent of young adults, and 6 percent of older adults had used hallucinogens.[24]

This national survey was conducted during a period when the 1960-1979 trend of accelerated expansion in drug use in the United States had been somewhat reversed. The 1985 survey showed that this new trend had been blocked, however:

> Probably the most important discovery of 1985 is that the more or less constant decline of the last four years in total use of drugs among high school seniors seems to have halted.... This break in the long term trends was also confirmed in data on trends among college students and young adults in general.

> Simultaneous with this halt in the decline of total involvement with illegal drugs came an increased use of cocaine among high-school graduates in 1985.... Current use (during the 30 days previous to the survey) rose from 4.9% of those surveyed in 1983 to 5.8% in 1984 and to 6.7% in 1985 ... around 17% of all 1985 graduates had tried it....

> Not only do a good portion of graduates try cocaine, but the lifetime prevalence and active use increase dramatically when people reach their mid-twenties. Among people 27 years old, in the follow-up study, approximately 40%—four out of every ten

---

[24]Actual rates of use were registered as follows: 3.8 percent of young people, 7 percent of young adults, and 1.2 percent of older adults used cocaine; 1.4 percent of the young, 1.7 percent of young adults, and less than 0.5 percent of older adults used hallucinogens; heroin use was not reported. National Institute on Drug Abuse, *National Survey*, p. 14.

of these young adults—had tried cocaine (only 10%
of them had used cocaine when they were graduates in 1976).

The steady decline since 1979 in the use of marijuana among graduates levelled off in 1985. The
lifetime, annual, normal and daily prevalence now
remains at 54%, 41%, 26% and 4.9% respectively.
This halt is also observed among college students
and among the full sampling of young adults....

The three classes of illegal drugs which now have
a considerable impact on the U.S. young ... are
marijuana, cocaine and stimulants. Among high
school graduates surveyed in 1985, the annual
prevalence rates were 41%, 13% and 16% respectively. Among university students, the comparable
annual prevalence rates are 42%, 17% and 12%; and
for all high school graduates (the sampling of
young adults) the respective annual prevalence
rates are 41%, 20% and 14%....

The already high proportion of young people who
have tried at least one illegal drug by the time they
graduate from high school (61% in 1985) rises
substantially when they reach their mid-twenties
(reaching 75% to 85% in 1985) ... including around
50% to 55% who have tried an additional drug,
usually together with marijuana. Even for high
school graduates, these proportions range between
61% and 40% respectively.

Clearly, high school graduates and other young
adults of this nation still display a level of involvement with illegal drugs which is higher than levels in other industrialized countries. Even given the
historic patterns in this country, these ratios are
extremely high.[25]

   In terms of monetary value, these markets again produce huge
figures. Drug dealers gross up to $110 billion a year—2.9 percent
of U.S. GNP, double U.S. expenditures on oil and half of U.S.

---

[25]National Institute on Drug Abuse, *Drug Use*, pp. 13-14, 20. The cited quotation is
translated from a Spanish version of the original—*editor's note*.

military spending, according to official estimates.[26] These estimates have been questioned,[27] but even critics confirm that sales reach several dozen billions of dollars and that it most likely comes close to $100 billion.[28]

In summary, there are marked contrasts between the U.S. and Mexican drug markets. One is a massive market, the other a marginal one; one is the richest in the world, the other exceptionally poor; one is dominated by expensive drugs (heroin and cocaine), the other by less costly products; one is a growing market, the other, operating in an economy in crisis, is not; one is attractive to organized crime, the other to petty criminals and sometimes to established merchants who are willing to violate the law. Finally, the Mexican market is practically self-sufficient, while the U.S. market is highly dependent on imported raw materials and some foreign-based industrial and commercial processes. U.S. dependence on external supply is much more threatening to peace and health in Mexico than is Mexico's own national drug market.

Mexican Participation and Value Added

Independent of the social and cultural differences between Mexico and the United States, their three-thousand-kilometer border, their propitious ecosystems for cultivating marijuana and heroin, and Washington's erratic policies that once encouraged the licit production of morphine and marijuana in Mexico have all affected the binational illegal drug market. If Canada had Mexico's climate and geographic proximity to South American production, it surely would play as prominent a role in the export of illegal drugs to the United States as it did in the illegal export of alcohol during Prohibition.

---

[26]President's Commission on Organized Crime.

[27]Peter Reuter and Mark R. Kleiman make two major criticisms: "First, official estimates assume that all final sales occur at retail price. In fact, as the National Intelligence Commission on Drug Use now concedes (1983), a significant fraction of total sales of the most common units (Uqv. half an ounce of cocaines) are at prices very much below the retail level. Second, official estimates reflect unreal assumptions on the frequency of use by regular users and by dosage units." "Risks and Prices: An Economic Analysis of Drug Enforcement," *Crime and Justice*, July 1986, p. 295. This quotation is translated from a Spanish version of the original—*editor's note*.

[28]The high estimate comes from the National Organization for Regularization of Marijuana Laws (NORML), and the lower estimate from the National Drug Enforcement Policy Board Federal Law Enforcement Progress Report (mimeographed, March 1986), p. 9.

The United States is not officially considered a producer of heroin or cocaine (it does not have the necessary climatic conditions). It is an important producer of marijuana, however, particularly the highly potent "seedless" variety. Estimates of domestic marijuana production range from 12 to 51 percent of total market supply. The actual market share varies between these two extremes over time, depending on the effectiveness of campaigns to abolish production and to block the entry of marijuana from Colombia, Mexico, the Caribbean, and elsewhere.

The importance of the Mexican supply in the illegal U.S. drug market has tended to vary with climatic and political-military conditions in other marijuana-exporting countries (Colombia, Jamaica), with the heroin supply from the Middle East and Southeast Asia, and with the pressures the United States exerts on these countries to eradicate and intercept drugs directed to the U.S. market. Even though Mexico does not produce cocaine, traffic in this drug was diverted through Mexico when maritime controls on drugs entering Florida obstructed their entry there. Mexican heroin in the illegal U.S. drug market—according to official U.S. figures—accounted for 90 percent of supply (7.5 tons) in the mid-seventies (when Turkey decided to regulate its production and dramatic military events affected other producer countries in Southeast Asia) to 30 percent (1.5 tons) in the mid-eighties (when the supply of Asian heroin rose again). Estimates suggest that Mexican marijuana has fluctuated from around 50 percent of U.S. supply (five thousand tons when Colombian and Caribbean marijuana producers could not gain entry to the U.S. market and when the relative price of U.S. marijuana was high) to around 25 percent (twenty-five hundred tons, when Colombian marijuana flooded the U.S. market and Mexico's antidrug campaign raised the price and restricted the supply of Mexican marijuana vis-à-vis Colombian and domestic supplies.[29] A recent U.S. congressional report states that:

> since about 42% of the heroin, 35% of the marijuana and 33% of the cocaine consumed in the United States is either cultivated in or transported from Mexico, the United States cannot allow itself to reduce its vigilance on the anti-drug efforts within Mexico.[30]

[29]Del Villar, "La narcotización," pp. 73-77.
[30]99th Congress H.R., Select Committee on Narcotics Abuse and Control, *Annual Report 1985* (Washington, D.C.: U.S. Government Printing Office, 1986), p. 67.

Interestingly, fluctuations in the supply of illegal drugs from Mexico do not affect patterns of drug use in the United States. However, Mexican supply is of utmost relevance to other suppliers. Even more interesting, the U.S. House of Representatives' Select Commission on Drug Abuse and Control expresses no interest in its report in overseeing how the U.S. government controls domestic drug producers in the United States (calculated at four million who produce for their own use and 200-500 thousand who produce for the retail market). The commission's report does not even mention this issue. Also noteworthy is the fact that the commission devotes less than two pages of its seventy-three-page report to massive drug use in the United States. The lack of concern about what goes on within the U.S. drug market is frankly inexplicable, especially since the big drug business and the organizations that benefit from it are located in this country. The U.S. drug market leaves practically nothing in Mexico relative to what it leaves in the United States. On the basis of Reuter and Kleiman's adaptation of figures from the National Intelligence Commission on Drug Use in the United States, of each dollar paid by marijuana users, between ninety-one and ninety-three cents remain in the United States. The same is true of cocaine, where ninety-seven to ninety-nine cents remain in the United States; the figure for heroin is ninety-five to ninety-six cents. Agricultural producers in countries like Mexico, Peru, Jamaica, Thailand, Turkey, and Pakistan see only a fraction of a cent for each dollar paid by consumers in the United States.[31]

This appears to replicate the cruelest nineteenth-century imperialism, when center countries maximized their exploitation of suppliers of tropical raw materials and monopolized markets by regions. This characterization might be somewhat exaggerated but it is not that farfetched in light of the protectionism that effectively results from this market's regulatory, penal, and enforcement framework.

---

[31]A kilo of pure heroin (in 1980 prices) retailed for between $1.6 and $2.2 million, of which 13.75 and 10.91 percent, respectively, were paid at the import level, 5.94 and 4.32 percent at the export level, 0.38 and 0.45 percent for processing, and 0.022 and 0.045 percent on agricultural production. The estimated price of cocaine includes payment of 7.69 percent at the import level, 1.08 to 3.08 percent at the export level, 0.46 to 2.54 percent for processing, and 0.2 to 1.54 percent on agricultural production. A kilo of pure marijuana was estimated to cost between $1,250 and $2,090 on the market, with a payment of between 29.2 and 34.45 percent at the import level, 7.2 and 8.61 percent at the export level, 4.4 percent for processing, and 0.56 and 0.86 percent on agricultural production. Reuter and Kleiman, "Risks and Prices," p. 293.

THE LEGAL RESPONSE

It makes no sense to separate the analysis of Mexico's govern-
mental-legal response to the illegal narcotics market from the U.S.
response. They are as intertwined as the two countries' drug
markets, even though this interrelationship may be embarrassing,
difficult, costly, counterproductive, and occasionally violent.

The Legal Framework and Drug Traffic

Basically, Mexico's legal response to drug traffic began in 1912
when it signed the International Opium Convention in The Hague.
The agreement specified that:

> signing parties will examine the possibility of
> enacting laws or regulations to make illegal the
> possession of raw opium, the opium prepared from
> morphine, from cocaine and its respective salts,
> unless the subject matter has been regulated by
> existing laws or regulations.[32]

Since the Mexican Revolution the Mexican government has
fought drug traffic with all the resources available, even accept-
ing international legal-administrative guidelines (formulated
essentially by the U.S. government) that have been extremely costly
for the nation. In 1927 President Plutarco Elías Calles subscribed
to the Hague Convention, the 1931 code of which remains in effect.[33]

In 1961, the Mexican government signed the Sole Convention
on Narcotics drawn up at the United Nations that same year—again
in response to U.S. government pressure. The convention was
approved by the Mexican Senate in December 1966 and implemented by President Gustavo Díaz Ordaz in April 1967 as a basic
component of Mexican law.[34] The core of the agreement was that
signatories were obliged to penalize any participation in the value-
added chain of narcotics supply:

---

[32]International Opium Convention, signed in The Hague, 23 January 1912, Article
19. Mexico subscribed to the Convention on 16 May 1912.
[33]For a historical view of Mexico's legal treatment of drug traffic from the 1871
"Martínez de Castro" criminal code and the change wrought by the 1929 "Almaraz"
code through 1931 and the Convention of The Hague, see Heredia Jasso Carlos,
"Consideraciones legales sobre las drogas y la sociedad mexicana," in *Las drogas y
la sociedad mexicana* (Mexico: INISS, 1970), pp. 51-57.
[34]"Decreto del 22 de abril de 1967 por el que se promulga el texto de la Convención
Unica de 1961 sobre Estupefacientes," *Diario Oficial de la Federación*, 25 April 1962.

Apart from the provisions of their Constitution, each of the parties undertakes to all such measures so that the cultivation and production, manufacture, extraction, preparation, possession, general offer, sales offer, distribution, purchase, sale, dispatch in any form, brokerage, issue, transit, transport or import of narcotics not in accordance with the provisions of this Convention, or any other acts which in the opinion of the party can effectuate in a violation of the provisions of this Convention, will be deemed to be crimes if intentionally committed and the serious crimes will be penalized adequately, particularly with prison sentences or other freedom-depriving penalties.[35]

Particular emphasis was placed on poppy, coca leaves, and cannabis. A safeguard was also provided to depenalize possession and, consequently, tolerate use (i.e., demand): "The parties will only allow possession of narcotics with legal authorization." Furthermore, it stipulated noncriminal treatment for users: "The parties will make special consideration of such measures as may be adopted for the medical treatment, care and rehabilitation of drug addicts."

The 1961 convention organized national as well as international models for regulating the drug market. This had a very real effect on the evolution of the market, particularly the U.S. market which conditions drug traffic in Mexico. Essentially, it set up a dual legal-governmental response to the phenomenon: a repression of supply and a tolerance for demand, setting the groundwork for the spectacular growth of the illegal U.S. drug market in the 1960s and 1970s, a corrupting and uncontrollable flow of drug dollars toward Mexico, and the coming of major crime organizations that control the flow. The Vietnam War and its impact on U.S. culture generated a massive market, the richest in the world, of tolerated consumers. By making the supplying of drugs a crime, the 1961 convention reserved the drug business for criminals. The United States' international drug control program and its impacts on producer countries have caused narcotics prices and profits to rise

---

[35]"Convención de 1961," Article 36. Additionally, in 1962 a reform protocol of the convention was signed along with a new convention on psychotropic substances. See Congressional Research Service, Library of Congress, *Compilation of Narcotics Laws, Treaties, and Executive Documents*, Committee on Foreign Affairs, 99 H. R. (Washington, D.C.: U.S. Government Printing Office), pp. 203-224.

to inordinate levels along with the dimensions of the market and increased the incentives for crime companies to expand their operations.

The convention's regulatory framework also provides a two-sided pattern for treating countries involved in the market. Supplier/producer countries are castigated, while countries characterized by consumer demand are treated with tolerance. Mexico's response to the convention has been to assemble an impressive police-military apparatus to eradicate and intercept drugs on their way to the United States and to penalize Mexicans—mainly peasants—who produce and sell drugs in the field. Mexico's criminal code was also amended to reflect the dual pattern of penalization of supply and tolerance of demand imposed by the 1961 convention.

The criminal aspects of drug traffic in Mexico are treated in Chapter I, Title seven, Book two of the Common Law Criminal Code[36] which assigns to the federal government exclusive responsibility to "enact laws on ... general health in the Republic."[37] Chapter I address "production, holding, transit, promotion, and other matters with respect to narcotics and psychotropics," and Title 7 corresponds to the special "crimes against health" section of the criminal code. It comprises seven articles which define and classify narcotic and psychotropic drugs in accordance with health legislation and the 1961 international convention. They also set six levels of penalties, depenalize limited possession by addicts, and order the confiscation of narcotic and psychotropic drugs.[38]

The penalties,[39] in ascending order of seriousness by crime, are

- Two months to two years imprisonment and a fine of five hundred to one thousand pesos

  — for anyone who acquires or possesses for personal use prohibited narcotics or psychotropic drugs, if the quantity does not exceed that necessary for immediate and personal use.

---

[36]"Código Penal para el Distrito y Territorio Federales en materia del Fuero Común y para toda la República en materia del Fuero Federal del 13 de agosto de 1931," *Diario Oficial de la Federación*, 14 August 1931, amended by decree, 2 January 1968 (*Diario Oficial*, 8 March 1968).
[37]Constitución Política de los Estados Unidos Mexicanos, 15 February 1957, Article 73, Section 16.
[38]"Código Penal," Articles 193-199.
[39]The following paragraphs draw upon Title 7, Articles 194-197 and 297.

- Six months to three years in prison and a fine of up to fifteen thousand pesos

  — for any person not addicted to any of the prohibited narcotic or psychotropic drugs who acquires or possesses them one time only for personal use and in an amount not in excess of that necessary for his personal and immediate consumption.

- Two to six years in prison and a fine of two to twenty thousand pesos

  — for any person who acquires or possesses for personal use prohibited narcotic and psychotropic drugs to satisfy his personal need for a maximum of three days, but who in addition supplies them without charge to a third party ... for the personal use of the latter and in a quantity not in excess of that needed for his personal and immediate use.

- Two to eight years in prison and a fine of one to twenty thousand pesos

  — for any person who, on behalf of or financed by third parties, plants, cultivates, or harvests cannabis or marijuana plants, provided that such individual receives only minimal instruction and has extreme economic need.

  — for any person who allows, under the same circumstances as in the previous case, said plants to be cultivated on a piece of land owned, held, or possessed by him.

  — for any person who, not being a member of a criminal association, transports cannabis or marijuana, one single time, provided that the amount does not exceed one gram.

  — for the mere possession of cannabis or marijuana when because of the amount or actions involved, it cannot be established that there is an intent to carry out the crimes with maximum penalties. The fine in this case ranges from five to twenty-five thousand pesos.

- Seven to fifteen years imprisonment and a fine of ten thousand to one million pesos (without the right to bail guaranteed by Article 20 of the Constitution)

  — for any person who illegally plants, cultivates, harvests, manufactures, produces, elaborates, prepares, conditions, possesses—for more than three days' supply for personal use—transports, sells, buys, acquires, disposes of, or in any way traffics with, markets, supplies (even without charge), or prescribes prohibited narcotic or psychotropic drugs.

— for any person who illegally brings illegal drugs into or out of the country, even momentarily or in transit, or commits any act intended to consummate such acts.

— for any public official or employee who allows or covers up any of the foregoing acts for individuals intending to carry them out.

— for any person who contributes economic or any in-kind resources or in any way collaborates in financing the performance of any of the crimes referred to in this chapter.

— for any person who carries out acts of publicity, propaganda, general provocation, promotion, instigation, or illegal assistance intended to cause another to consume any prohibited drugs.

• The penalties are greater by one-third:

— if the agent takes advantage of his position or authority over the person instigated, induced, or helped to use prohibited substances.

— when any of the crimes mentioned in this chapter are committed by public servants acting in connection with the exercise of or by virtue of their obligations.

— when the victim is a minor, incompetent, or for whatever reason cannot resist the guidance of the agent.

— when committed in education centers or penitentiaries or in their immediate vicinities. (There are additional penalties of license revocation for medical practitioners and companies that commit any of the above crimes.)

Mexican criminal legislation clearly reflects the 1961 convention's differential treatment of demand and supply, although the safeguard of decriminalization of demand is still restricted to those cases where the user is not an addict or habitual user and when the quantity involved is not greater than that needed for personal or immediate use. Although the addict or habitual user is treated as a criminal when the quantity he acquires or possesses is greater than that required to satisfy his needs for a maximum term of three days, the penalty is still relatively minimal. When the addict or habitual user acquires or possesses a quantity in excess of a three-day supply, he becomes subject to the same penalties as a supplier.

Marijuana possession, transportation, and especially cultivation are treated differently than these same activities when they relate to other drugs, and participation in the international drug market and the domestic market are also viewed differentially. There is a tacit legislative acknowledgement of marijuana's lesser threat and of the injustice of treating the peasants who cultivate it as drug dealers. There is also a legislative recognition of the greater danger inherent in the international market. The mere intent to import or export narcotics and the covering up of such an intent by corrupt public servants are crimes in themselves.

The Administrative-Fiscal Framework

The prosecution of drug traffic in Mexico is paradoxically both highly centralized and decentralized. Two constitutional provisions support centralization. First, the investigation and prosecution of crimes against health are the legal responsibility of the attorney general. These duties fall under exclusive federal jurisdiction by virtue of the powers of the Mexican Congress to legislate on health matters. In other words, state governments and their law enforcement services do not have jurisdiction in these matters except as "assistants." Second, the federal and state judicial police—charged with maintaining public safety and subordinate to the *ministerio público* (federal prosecutor)—hold sole jurisdiction over official criminal investigations.[40] The other federal, state, and municipal police services supposedly only have jurisdiction for preventive functions (i.e., vigilance) and are prohibited from detaining criminals except in "flagrant" cases.[41] Many federal police services—

---

[40]This exclusivity is derived directly from the Constitution, which establishes that "prosecution of crimes is the duty of the Ministerio Público and the judicial police which are under its authority and immediate command." This provision holds for federal and general matters. As to exclusivity of the Ministerio Público Federal, headed by the Attorney General of the Republic, "he is charged . . . with the prosecution, in court, of all federal crimes; consequently, it is his responsibility to request detention orders against guilty parties; to seek and present evidence that proves the responsibility of the latter"; Constitution, Articles 214-102. The political constitutions of the states repeat this exclusivity for the prosecution of common crimes.

[41]This is in keeping with constitutional guarantees that "no one may be molested in his person, family, home, papers, or possessions, except by virtue of a written order from a competent authority. No detention or apprehension order may be issued except by the judicial authorities . . . except that anyone may apprehend a criminal

immigration, customs, highway police, and forest rangers—have no investigative powers, even though their preventive jurisdictions expose them to drug traffic. State governments are also powerless to respond to the regional peculiarities of these crimes. Furthermore, city governments retain no prosecutorial capacity whatever, irrespective of the incidence of these criminal activities in their territories and townships.

The concomitant decentralization of prosecutorial responsibilities arises from the identification of all law enforcement and justice services in the country as "assistants" to the federal *ministerio público*. They not only assist the federal prosecutor during investigation of drug traffic but also place at his disposal the evidence of crimes discovered while carrying out their crime prevention services (and investigation services in the case of state judicial police, which obviously includes surveillance). The policy of the attorney general has been to encourage this assistance from all police services because "fighting drug traffic implies a necessary and constant coordination between local authorities," based on a framework of "coordination agreements—initiated in 1984—between the federal and state governments in law enforcement matters."[42]

Within this very centralized law enforcement framework, Mexico's attorney general has a much wider range of responsibilities for the investigation and prosecution of crimes than his counterpart in the U.S. Department of Justice. In Mexico, legislative powers are interstate drug traffic and municipal governments' investigative powers all extremely helpful in the investigation and prosecution of drug crimes. On the other hand, the Office of the Attorney General has not gained fiscal priority. It is one of the poorest federal agencies, with a bare minimum of human, material, and technical resources with which to address its wide gamut of federal legal responsibilities. Furthermore, imbalances in Mexico's public finances resulting from state companies operating inefficiently have reduced its budget further.

---

and his accomplices, placing them without delay at the disposition of the nearest authorities. Only in urgent cases, when there is no judicial authority to be found, and in the case of crimes that are prosecuted *ex oficio*, may the administrative authority, under the strictest accountability, order the detention of an accused criminal, placing him immediately at the disposition of the judicial authorities." Article 16 of the Constitution.

[42]"Comunicado del Procurador General de la República y los procuradores generales de justicia de los estados del 6 de junio de 1986 expedido en la Ciudad de Campeche." See Procuraduría General de la República, *Campaña*, p. 473.

Despite these difficulties, the eradication and interception of drugs destined for U.S. consumption and the investigation and prosecution of related crimes consume the greater part of the resources of the Office of the Attorney General. Mexican efforts to eradicate and intercept drugs headed for the U.S. market represent the most significant police-military enterprise in Mexico over the last forty years. It began in 1946 with a campaign to destroy poppy fields in Sinaloa and evolved into a yearly campaign timed with the reproductive cycles of poppy and cannabis. Eventually it covered practically all of Mexico's territory.

It became a "permanent campaign" in the 1970s and its present proportions are enormous. The campaign's direct costs rose drastically—accounting for 41, 47, and 60 percent of the attorney general's entire budget for 1985, 1986 and 1987, respectively.[43] These costs included neither the impact of the campaign on the fixed expenses of the Attorney General's Office nor the cost of prosecuting drug crimes.

The U.S. government has contributed to the campaign, providing fifty-four helicopters and twenty-eight planes for identifying fields, transferring personnel to the fields, and spraying herbicides (including paraquat, which is prohibited in the United States). These supports totaled $86.9 million between 1976 and 1986. Most of the labor for these efforts was provided by the Mexican army. The defense minister calculates that "the current Mexican military administration has allotted the equivalent of $194.3 million dollars (up to April 1987) to finance operations against drug traffic," apart from the costs accrued in associated naval operations. The campaign occupied some 20 generals, 120 chiefs, 1,225 officers, and 25,000 troops, with an approximate daily per-soldier cost of $20, according to Mexican military estimates.[44] This would translate to a direct cost for the Mexican army of about a half million dollars (750 million pesos at the August 1987 exchange rate) per day for eradicating drugs destined basically for the United States. This estimate does not include costs and the additional effects of the campaign on the country's thirty-six military zones and the army's

[43]Supervisión General de Servicios Técnicos y Criminalísticos, Procuraduría General de la República, El Esfuerzo de México 1985-1986-1987 (Mexico: P.G.R., 1987), pp. 10-11.
[44]Juan Arévalo Gardoqui, Secretario de la Defensa Nacional, El Ejército Mexicano en la Campaña contra el Narcotráfico, presentation at the U.S. Department of Defense, Washington, D.C., 22 April 1987 (Mexico, D.F.: Procuraduría General de la República, 1987), p. 13.

central command. This disproportionate allocation of funds for the eradication of drugs destined for the United States must have equally disproportionate opportunity costs in terms of complying with the army's own objectives for expanding its services to ensure the security of Mexicans.[45]

Two additional considerations are the cost of coordinating the campaign with federal and local authorities in each state[46] and the cost of the "assistance" normally rendered by the federal *ministerio público* in prosecuting international drug crimes. These costs are undoubtedly higher than those associated with preventing or prosecuting any other crime affecting the Mexican population.

The campaign's basic objectives are to identify, intercept, and destroy narcotics. It is not designed to identify, investigate, or try criminals, nor does it seek intelligence on criminal organizations. Nonetheless, the attorney general incurs costs related to these activities as well. These included 7,849 preliminary investigations in 1976, 9,735 arrests, and 9,139 trials[47] to penalize drug crimes linked to the U.S. drug market. The pressures and additional costs imposed on the overburdened penal system, social rehabilitation services, and reformatories in Mexico are extraordinary.

As to the results of these efforts, the attorney general reports:[48]

- In 1986, 24,426 marijuana fields were destroyed over an area of 2,970 hectares, as compared to 17,675 fields over 1,738 hectares in 1985; seizures of marijuana by-products (dried plants, hashish, and seeds) amounted to 193.6 tons (compared to 174.2 tons in 1985). It should be noted that reported seizures between January and May 1987 amounted to 259.2 tons.

- In 1986, 24,823 poppy fields were destroyed (compared to 23,101 in 1985) over a surface of 2,383 hectares (2,297 in 1985); derivatives (opium, morphine, heroin, and seeds) reached 301.7 kilos (compared to 200.5 in 1985 and 109.7 from January to May 1987).

- With regard to cocaine, 5.3 tons were seized in 1986, compared to 2.6 tons in 1985, 2.3 tons in the entire decade from 1975-1984, and 3.2 tons from January to May 1987.

---

[45]See David F. Ronfeldt, *The Modern Mexican Military*, Monograph Series, no. 15 (La Jolla, Calif.: Center for U.S.-Mexican Studies, University of California, San Diego, 1984), p. 3.
[46]Procuraduría General, *Campaña*, p. 37.
[47]Ibid., pp. 436-439.
[48]Procuraduría General, *El Esfuerzo*, pp. 14-27.

The army reported the following outcome from its separate operations between December 1, 1982 and April 17, 1987:[49]

- The destruction of 198,000 marijuana fields planted on a total of 73,080 acres, "preventing the production of 40,579 long tons of the drug ... with a capacity to intoxicate 589 million persons in one week."

- The destruction of 324,646 poppy fields planted over 75,484 acres, "preventing the production of 673,505 pounds of heroin ... with a potential capacity to intoxicate 122.2 million persons in one week."

- Regarding cocaine, "4,636 tons have been destroyed ... with a potential capacity to intoxicate 420,660 persons in one week."

The Secretary of Defense emphasizes that,

> This ministry considers as truly worthwhile the fact that, with the destruction of all the drugs referred to, the potential intoxication of 711 million persons in one week was prevented.... The price of these drugs on the black market can be calculated at $151.195 billion.... 17,572 Mexican individuals and 101 foreigners have been detained as alleged drug dealers and placed at the disposition of the corresponding civil authorities.

Costs, Benefits, and Options

The results reported by the Attorney General's Office and the Ministry of Defense are very impressive. But more important, how much progress has there been in reducing the illegal drug market over forty years of increasing and unparalleled Mexican political, legal, and administrative efforts which basically serve to benefit the United States? The answer is, none. In July 1987, U.S. Ambassador to Mexico James Pilliod acknowledged that "we continue to lose the war against drugs."[50] Preliminary U.S. government reports corroborate once again that the quantity of drugs demanded from

---

[49]Arévalo Gardoqui, *El Ejército Mexicano*, pp. 12-13.
[50]Charles J. Pilliod, presentation at the Seventh Annual Briefing Session for Journalists, Center for U.S.-Mexican Studies, University of California, San Diego, La Jolla, California, 9 July 1987.

Mexico by the U.S. market continues to outpace these efforts and their impressive results and that this demand increases despite a string of forty-seven bilateral accords between Mexico and the United States on the subject of drug control.[51]

Some U.S. assessments on the U.S. government's international narcotics program are worthy of note:

> Despite the efforts of the U.S. and other governments to create an international moral standard on drugs, a true consensus does not exist, either in the United States or in the world. The drug problem is not a sickness like smallpox, in which everyone agrees on the need for its eradication. Nor can drug traffic be legitimately compared with the traffic of slaves. The eradication of this illegal traffic was made possible, in good measure, by a moral consensus against slavery. It is improbable that a moral consensus yet exists against the use of illegal drugs. And while individuals see no or very slight evil in using illegal drugs, there cannot be a true international consensus with respect to the immorality of drug traffic.[52]

> During the twentieth century, the U.S. government has maintained that the solution to the problem of drug addition in the United States is in the hands of the foreign countries that produce the most important illegal drugs. This perspective has been sustained by administrations as different as those of John Kennedy and Ronald Reagan, and for drugs as different as heroin and marijuana.... Unfortunately, there is abundant evidence that the external policies adopted by the United States for the control of drugs have failed.... The failures of U.S. international programs are not the result of incompetency or inadequate resources; they are found inherently in the structure of the problem.... They

---

[51]Congressional Research Service, Compilation of Narcotics Laws, pp. 231-241.
[52]Ethan Nadelman, "The Real International Drug Problem," presented at the conference on International Drugs: Threat and Response, Defense Intelligence Analysis Center, Bolling Air Force Base, Washington, D.C., 2 June 1987.

will do very little to reduce drug abuse in the
United States.[53]

Both the public and the government in the United
States should acknowledge that drug use in that
country is above all an internal matter. It is useless
and counterproductive to try to find a solution to
the problem in other countries. That only provokes
resentment among foreign nations, antagonizes or
belittles governments that should be friends, and
seriously complicates and compromises U.S. foreign policy. Washington's international antidrug
campaign is a poorly conceived irremediable failure that should be abolished without delay.[54]

Essentially, the structural failure of U.S. international drug-
control policy, which influences Mexico's drug policies through the
structure of bilateral accords, leaves Mexico with two options. It
can allot even more funds to carry out these policies, or it can
initiate a process for revising the mistaken, inequitable, and
counterproductive premises on which they are based.

It is obvious that the first of these options eventually would
lead to chaos. A Mexican government that increasingly assigns the
bulk of its law enforcement, public security, and even national
security apparatus to eradicate and intercept drugs destined for
the tolerated and even economically protected U.S. market, that
employs this apparatus to repress the largely campesino population that responds to that demand, and that increasingly exposes
that apparatus to the corrupting flow of drug dollars would eventually lose its legitimacy. Mexico's government must respond to
its foundation—the people of Mexico and their security, not to the
U.S.'s international drug-control program or the bureaucracy and
policies that feed on it.

Structural changes in a century-old national and international
political, legal, and administrative apparatus will not come easily.
Nevertheless, there appears to be no alternative. By continuing

---

[53]Peter Reuter, "Eternal Hope: America's International Narcotics Effort" (Santa
Monica, Calif.: Rand Corporation, February 1987).
[54]Ted Galen Carpenter, "The U.S. Campaign against International Narcotics
Trafficking: A Cure Worse than the Disease," mimeo. (Washington, D.C.: The Cato
Institute, 9 December 1985).

present policies the Mexican government would only continue to stimulate—through high prices and higher profits—the illegal drug market and the corruption that accompanies it.

To facilitate the needed structural changes, I offer possible guidelines for domestic, bilateral, and multilateral actions.[55] Essentially, they involve constructing a new antidrug policy based on the following premises:

- A recognition that acts of government coercion in a constitutional regime with guarantees of freedom cannot substitute for individual moral decisions. An attempt to make such a substitution only leads to the emergence of black markets and the delinquency and corruption that feed on them. The drug market is a most dramatic example.

- A reordering of priorities in the allocation of government funds for drug control—toward demand—thus broadening the options for treatment and rehabilitation.

- A distinction between the very various drugs, and a redefinition of the legal-institutional treatment corresponding to each one.

- Finally, a reordering of priorities regarding legal and political efforts—away from massive coercion in the countryside, on the borders, and toward the suppliers and/or small demanders of low-toxicity drugs on the streets, and toward the development of government organizations capable of bringing big organized crime to justice.

---

[55]Del Villar, "La narcotización."

Appendix:
Production and Supply of Drugs

Miguel Ruiz-Cabañas I.

THE INTERNATIONAL SUPPLY OF ILLICIT DRUGS

Effective policy requires accurate knowledge, and this does not exist. The first problem we face in calculating the total international supply of illicit drugs is the lack of data. The cultivation, manufacture, and trafficking of illicit drugs are by definition illicit activities. Producers, exporters/importers, wholesalers, and dealers do not report to the governments on their activities and they do not pay taxes.

We are left, then, with the possibility of obtaining data only through *indirect* means, which cannot give an entirely clear picture. Theoretically, there are several possibilities for means of estimation:

- Figures or estimates of illicit cultivation on those countries where the drugs are produced. These estimates would give us the amount of the *potential production*. These amounts, however, are far from being the international supply because in order to obtain the *net production* we have to take into account the results of eradication programs. We should also discount the operational losses, domestic consumption, and seizures to obtain the *net international supply*. We are not in a position to obtain these estimates, regrettably, because most countries do not have data on either illicit cultivation or losses and domestic consumption.

- Indicators of the consequences of the consumption of the various types of illicit drugs (data from hospital emergency rooms, medical examiners' offices, and drug treatment facilities) and surveys of drug habits among the general population or specific groups. Some of these data, which refer to the habit and results of drug abuse, are produced systematically only in a few developed countries. Being indirect data on the magnitude of the demand, they are only complementary to data focusing on the supply side.

- Indicators of the results of law enforcement activities (number of individuals arrested, quantities of drugs and assets seized, conveyances from which seizures were made). Most countries, at least those most affected by the production, trafficking, and consumption of illicit drugs, obtain some of these figures and report them to the United Nations, albeit with many gaps and doubts about their reliability.

Complementing these possibilities, we could also make some estimates of the supply of an illicit drug (in a specific market and at a given moment) by observing the movements in its price. But we must keep in mind that the price of the drug is affected by law enforcement activities. The relative price of a drug is always the result of demand and the net production that is exported, less seizures. Besides, with the probable exception of the United States, there is no country that has systematically recorded the prices of illicit drugs in its markets. Apparently, only certain agencies of the U.S. government work to produce statistics on production and supply for various countries.[1] The possibility of presenting accurate figures on the international supply of illicit drugs is therefore limited. At most, we can deduce some general trends by observing some existing data—such as the amounts of seizures made every year—and combining our analysis with other data on consumption levels.

The United Nations, through its Division on Narcotic Drugs, has since 1947 recorded the total quantities of illicit drugs reported to have been seized throughout the world. These figures have been provided by governments in accordance with their obligations

---

[1]See the annual reports of the Bureau of International Narcotics Matters of the U.S. Department of State, *International Narcotics Control Strategy Report*, or the annual reports of the National Narcotics Intelligence Consumers Committee (NNICC), *The Supply of Illicit Drugs to the United States from Foreign and Domestic Sources (With Near Term Projections)*. The last of these reports, covering 1985-1986, was published in June 1987.

under existing international conventions for controlling the production and trafficking of illicit drugs. This is the only indicator
available that has been systematically recorded for all geographical regions. For these practical reasons, we have chosen it to analyze
the general trends of the international supply of illicit drugs,
bearing in mind that it is an indicator of trafficking trends and only
indirectly of production trends.[2]

It has been argued that seizures tend to represent around 10
percent of the total quantity of drugs not interdicted and eventually consumed. As plausible as this assumption may appear, there
is no basis for applying it indiscriminately. This could be the actual
situation at times, but at other times the amount of seizures could
represent a proportion as high as 50 percent or as low as 5 percent. This is so because law enforcement activities can produce very
different outcomes. For example, tough law enforcement could
result in a temporary lowering of the quantities seized, precisely
because traffickers will not attempt to challenge it. Other times,
however, stronger measures against traffickers might result in
greater countermeasures by them, developing not only new routes
and methods of smuggling, but spreading more violence and corruption. On the other hand, seizures of greater quantities of drugs
may indeed represent an increase in the supply and, paradoxically,
greater effectiveness by the traffickers if, at the same time, no significant lowering of the consumption levels is observed.[3]

Worldwide Seizures of Illicit Drugs

With these reservations in mind, we can observe the total
quantities of the main illicit drugs reported seized worldwide from
1947 to 1985, as reported to the United Nations (tables 1-5).

Table 1 chronicles a continuous increase in the seizures of
cannabis herbs, plants, and resin, and a certain stabilization in the
seizures of cannabis liquid. We should stress the dramatic increase
that the seizures show after 1975. In this year the seizures of the

---

[2]See United Nations, *Data on the Illicit Traffic in Narcotic Drugs and Psychotropic
Substances during 1985. Note by the Secretary General.* Document presented to the
Commission on Narcotic Drugs, thirty-second session, Vienna, Austria, 2-11 February 1987, U.N. doc.E/CN.7/1987/CRP.6.
[3]For an analysis of this problem and of the problems with the lack of data in this
area, see Mark Kleiman, "Data and Analysis Requirements for Policy toward Drug
Enforcement and Organized Crime," in *America's Habit: Drug Abuse, Drug Trafficking and Organized Crime,* President's Commission on Organized Crime, Appendix
G (Washington: U.S. Government Printing Office, 1986).

Table 1. Cannabis Seizures Worldwide

Yearly Average	Herb/Plants kg	Resin kg	Liquid kg
1947-1966	342,370[a]		
1967-1974	2,335,354	45,877	336[b]
Year			
1975	3,138,292	60,942	451
1976	1,904,650	77,309	508
1977	3,149,912	164,825	1,084
1978	6,384,791	172,344	699
1979	6,100,730	131,952	1,592
1980	5,805,929	171,750	1,121
1981	5,299,735	291,493	1,274
1982	7,295,095	222,427	694
1983	11,719,378	278,245	925
1984	25,803,613	309,384	1,044
1985	6,483,895	360,544	543

Note: Amounts reported in liters in tables 1-5 are included in weights reported in kilograms.

[a]Including plants and resin.

[b]Representing the average for three years, no seizures having been reported before 1971.

Source, tables 1-7 and figures 1-5: United Nations, *Data on the Illicit Traffic in Narcotic Drugs and Psychotropic Substances during 1985. Note by the Secretary General*, U.N. document E/CN.7/1987/CRP.6 pp. 5-9, 51-55.

three types of cannabis surpass the amount of seizures from the eight preceding years. We can also observe a tendency to obtain lower seizures in the years following periods of high amounts seized. This is the case for cannabis herbs and plants in 1976, and markedly in 1985. It is also the case for cannabis resin in 1979 and 1982. It is impossible to affirm whether those tendencies were due to traffickers' caution in response to tough law enforcement in a given year, or to some other factor.

Table 2 presents trends in the amount of cocaine seizures similar to those observed in table 1. Indeed, the amount of seizures increases dramatically in 1975 (2,407 kg), 1980 (11,820 kg) and in particular after 1983 (41,005 kg). In 1985 the amount of seizures (56,243 kg) was also one hundred times greater than the seizures for the entire eight-year period from 1967 to 1974, and five times more than the seizures made in 1980 (11,820 kg).

Table 3 offers similar trends in increased amounts of seizures of opium and heroin. Again, the increases in heroin seizures were enormous from 1975 (1,708 kg) to 1985 (14,115 kg). Seizures of opium descended in 1984 (59,493 kg) and 1985 (40,738 kg), after having reached a record 82,420 kg in 1983. In the case of morphine

Table 2. Cocaine Seizures Worldwide

Yearly Average	Cocaine kg
1947-1966	41
1967-1974	625
Year	
1975	2,406
1976	2,419
1977	3,977
1978	5,391
1979	8,365
1980	11,820
1981	9,541
1982	12,113
1983	41,005
1984	59,404
1985	56,243

Table 3. Opiates Seizures Worldwide

Yearly Average	Opium kg	Morphine kg	Heroin kg	Other kg	Opiates units[a]
1947-1966	41,845	264	187	—	
1967-1974	44,162	1,072	953	—	
Year					
1975	31,220	399	1,708	6	249
1976	50,969	695	2,586	171	12,443
1977	38,416	564	2,377	3	4,132
1978	43,617	521	2,441	4	2,804
1979	70,324	604	2,070	361	17,880
1980	51,786	1,495	2,510	34	453,666
1981	54,452	1,906	5,613	5	11,241
1982	45,756	2,201	6,210	10	124
1983	83,470	1,618	11,827	2	3,444
1984	59,493	449	10,643	3	1,326
1985	40,738	522	14,145	10	1,499

[a]Units include doses, ampuls, injections, phials, tablets, etc.

there was a continuous increase in the amount of seizures from 1975 (399 kg) to 1982 (2,201 kg).

The trends in table 4 differ from those in tables 1, 2, and 3. In the case of depressants, there was a definitive trend toward increased seizures until 1981 (24 kg and 23 million units). Seizures then decreased in 1982 and 1983 (512 kg and 3.7 million units). However, in 1984 and 1985 the trend again showed an increase (1,342 kg and 7 million units). In the case of stimulants, there was also a marked upward trend to 1981 (47.9 million units) and again in 1983 and 1984 (23.8 million units), with a decrease in 1985 (6.6 million units).

Table 4. Depressants and Stimulants Seized Worldwide

| Yearly average | Depressants[a] | | Stimulants | |
	kg	units[b]	kg	units[b]
1947-1966	—	—	—	—
1967-1974	193[c]	849,960[c]	241	5,775,978
Year				
1975	4,826	804,113	4,783	8,266,552
1976	12	1,366,514	281	6,579,941
1977	2,127	1,036,434	907	14,428,018
1978	3,861	517,672	584	22,152,331
1979	117	12,412,778	694	15,166,269
1980	2,654	25,324,609	736	30,680,119
1981	24,090	23,036,295	1,112	47,910,073
1982	1,656	12,773,238	1,474	4,953,695
1983	512	3,771,033	1,663	11,492,718
1984	2,069	4,679,949	8,728	23,824,876
1985	1,341	7,029,467	3,645	6,648,520

[a]Including methaqualone.

[b]Units include doses, ampuls, injections, phials, tablets, etc.

[c]This figure represents the average for six years, no seizures having been reported for 1967 and 1968.

Table 5 presents seizures of LSD and hallucinogens. In the case of the latter, the amount of seizures increased markedly in the late seventies and again in 1983 (452 kg and 3.4 million units). After an extreme reduction in 1984 (33 kg and 28,898 units) they increased in 1985 (812 kg and 1 million units). In the case of LSD, the most important seizures were made in 1975 (10.8 kg) and 1976 (11.6 kg). After these years, seizures of the drug descended until 1981 (0.110 kg). Since then, they have shown a continuous trend to increase (1.901 kg in 1985). Seizures of units of LSD, however, peaked in 1981 (36.3 million units), descended from 1982 to 1984, and showed a marked tendency to increase in 1985 (14.9 million units).

In general, the tables show steady increases in the amount of seizures made worldwide, in particular over the last five years. These increases were specially dramatic for cannabis (herb, plants, and resin), cocaine, and heroin.

Geographical Distribution of Worldwide Seizures

The geographical distribution of worldwide seizures has been uneven. The regions and countries most affected by the illicit cultivation, production, or consumption of drugs account for the most important amounts of seizures. This is the case for the Americas,

Table 5. Hallucinogens and LSD Seizures Worldwide

| Yearly Average | Hallucinogens | | LSD | |
	kg	units[a]	kg	units[a]
1947-1966	—	—	—	—
1967-1974	89.600[b]	3,845,020[b]	1.126	137,310
Year				
1975	106.715	2,492,120	10.802	206,283
1976	19.277	1,924,350	11.636	197,365
1977	15.826	4,129,328	8.438	95,917
1978	25.484	18,108,908	1.648	5,487,155
1979	68.825	9,900,382	4.031	228,070
1980	49.778	7,785,792	0.447	297,849
1981	12.987	45,747	0.110	36,305,692
1982	74.193	1,982,483	0.264	181,609
1983	452.204	3,418,533	0.800	3,199,114
1984	33.175	28,898	0.889	588,618
1985	812.192	1,085,322	1.091	14,942,079

[a]Units include doses, ampuls, injections, phials, tablets, etc.

[b]This figure represents the average for six years, no seizures having been reported for 1967 and 1968.

where more than 90 percent of cannabis herb and cocaine seizures have been made. It is also the case for heroin and opium, where the most significant seizures have taken place in the Near and Middle East (Afghanistan, Iran, Lebanon, Pakistan). This regional concentration of drug seizures can be appreciated in figures 1 to 5.

Figure 1 clearly shows the concentration of cannabis herb seizures in the Americas, especially in the last four years (1982-1985), when seizures averaged 91.7 percent. This percentage makes a surprising contrast with the less than 1 percent, on average, represented by European seizures over the last three years.

Figure 2 indicates the important participation of European and Near and Middle East seizures of cannabis resin. Considered together, they represented more than 75 percent, on average, of total seizures of this drug.

Figure 3, again, reveals the importance of the Americas. This region has accounted for practically all the important seizures of cocaine over the entire period. In the last four years the European region made some seizures, averaging less than 3 percent of the total.

There has been less regional concentration of heroin seizures, as can be noted in figure 4. The important seizures made in the Near and Middle East since 1980, after a period of limited participation

Figure 1. Quantities of Cannabis Herb Reported Seized Worldwide, 1975-1985

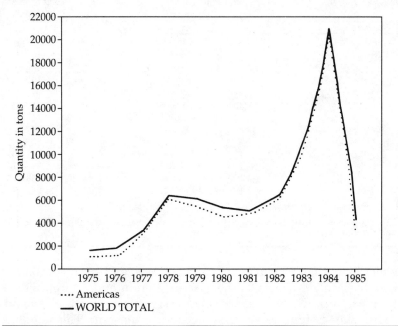

Figure 2. Quantities of Cannabis Resin Reported Seized Worldwide, 1975-1985

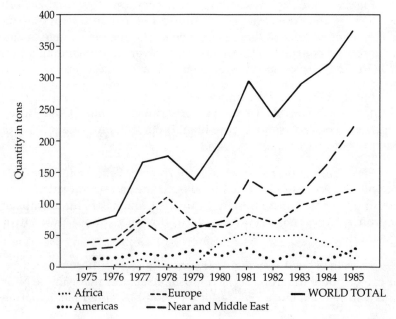

Figure 3. Quantities of Cocaine Reported Seized Worldwide, 1975-1985

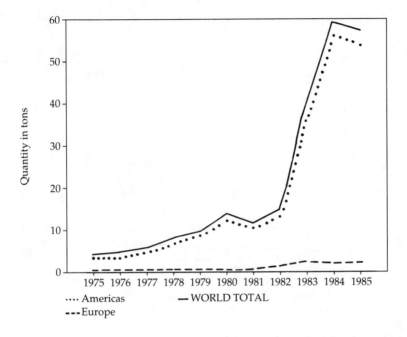

.... Americas   — WORLD TOTAL
---Europe

by this region, are significant. It is also important to note the relatively low amount of seizures made in the Americas, taking into account that the U.S. market is one of the most important in the world. Mexico is the only country in the region where opium reportedly is produced. Heroin laboratories have been destroyed there and in the United States for several years. There are two explanations, then, for the comparatively low amount of seizures in the Americas: 1) Mexican production is comparatively smaller than that of Southwest or Southeast Asia; 2) Mexican eradication programs have destroyed extensive zones of cultivation, before opium and heroin were produced.

Figure 5 shows the important concentration of opium seizures in the two most important producer zones: Southwest and Southeast Asia. Again, seizures in other regions—Europe and the Americas—have not been significant. This may be because opium as such is not widely consumed in those regions. Heroin, extracted from opium, is consumed instead (the proportion is approximately 10 kg of opium gum to 1 kg of heroin).

Figure 4. Quantities of Heroin Reported Seized Worldwide, 1975-1985

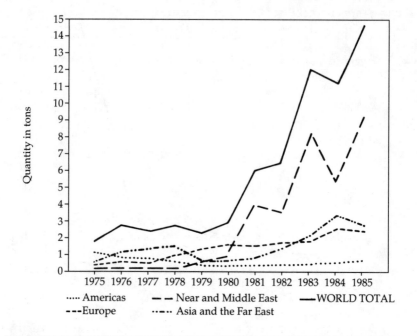

Figure 5. Quantities of Opium Reported Seized Worldwide, 1975-1985

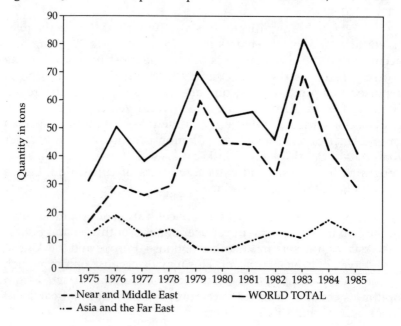

The regional concentration of seizures of certain drugs also indicates the particular concern of the governments of those areas with respect to the supply and consumption of certain types of drugs. This is the case with cannabis herb, cocaine, and, to a lesser extent, heroin in the Americas. It is also the case with heroin in the Near and Middle East, where seizures increased sharply in the early 1980s after addiction among the local population became a national problem in Iran and Pakistan. The same inference could be made for Europe (principally Western Europe), where there have been significant seizures but not of cannabis herb, a widely abused drug in the region.

Some Indicators of Consumption

Drug abuse grew significantly in the period 1975-85 in all the regions and countries affected. This is the case in the United States, Western Europe, the Near and Middle East, and Southeast Asia. These trends are stressed in the annual reports of the International Narcotics Control Board. Available data are fragmentary, but a few examples illustrate the point.

- In some Western European countries drug-related deaths increased dramatically. For the years 1973, 1975, 1979, 1980, and 1986, Denmark (population 5 million) reported 55, 61, 125, 105, and 158 drug-related deaths; the Federal Republic of Germany (population 62 million) reported 106, 188, 623, 410, and 152; Italy (population 56 million) reported 1, 26, 129, 145, and 237.[4]

- The number of heroin abusers reached half a million in 1986 in Pakistan, where the problem was considered insignificant ten years ago. In Iran, the number of opium abusers was calculated at half a million and heroin abusers at more than 100 thousand in 1985. In Burma, Malaysia, and Thailand, the number of heroin or opium addicts reached record levels of 60, 250, and 400 thousand, respectively.[5] In the United States, heroin abusers have leveled off at half a million since the mid-seventies, but cocaine

---

[4]The data for the years 1973 to 1980 were obtained from the INCB report for 1980, United Nations document E/INCB/52, p. 24. For the year 1986, see United Nations Economic and Social Council, Commission on Narcotic Drugs, *Review of Drug Abuse and Measures to Reduce Illicit Demand. Report by the Secretary General*, U.N. document E/CN.7/1987/9, pp. 19-21.
[5]See *International Narcotics Control Board Report for 1986*, United Nations document E/INCB/1986/1, pp. 18-23.

abuse has increased sharply, from 1.18 million abusers in 1975 to 5-6 million in 1986. In 1974 there were 12.4 million cannabis abusers in the United States while in 1985 the number increased to more than 20 million.[6]

In conclusion, worldwide increases in drug seizures have not been enough to ameliorate worldwide consumption. Obviously, these trends confirm that the international supply of illicit drugs has multiplied in the last ten years, along with demand and consumption. As a result of increased international supply and increased law enforcement activities, and in the absence of significant and durable reductions in the consumption levels, trafficking groups have probably become better organized and have greater resources than ever before. If so, more violence and corruption can be expected worldwide in the near future. Drug trafficking has become the most profitable illicit activity in the world. According to the prime minister of Malaysia, president of the International Conference on Drug Abuse and Illicit Trafficking recently celebrated in Vienna, worldwide illicit drug trade can be calculated at more than $300 billion.[7]

MEXICO'S PARTICIPATION IN WORLDWIDE SEIZURES

The Mexican participation in worldwide drug seizures appears in tables 6 and 7.

We can divide the years of cannabis seizures into three different periods. The first, from 1975 to 1978, is when Mexico embarked on a strong campaign against cultivation, production, and trafficking of illicit drugs. Mexico's cannabis seizures were extremely significant worldwide in those years (1975, 11.6 percent; 1976, 23 percent; 1977, 32.6 percent; 1978, 8 percent). The second stage, from 1979 to 1983, tends to present a reduced amount of seizures, less than 3 percent of worldwide seizures annually, probably due to the success achieved in the previous years. The third stage, 1984 and 1985, was peculiar. Seizures in 1984 represented 32.7 percent of the worldwide total, while 1985 showed a more "normal" participation of 2.5 percent. Trends in heroin and opium seizures have been different. Heroin seizures were very significant in the

---

[6]See President's Commission on Organized Crime, *America's Habit: Drug Abuse, Drug Trafficking and Organized Crime*, pp. 15-47.
[7]"Statement by President of International Conference on Drug Abuse and Illicit Trafficking," United Nations, Press Release ICDAIT/MISC/3, 17 June 1987, p. 2.

Table 6. Mexico: Seizures of Cannabis, Opium and Heroin[a] (total amounts and as percent of worldwide seizures)

Year	Cannabis		Opium		Heroin
	Herb	Seed	Herb	Seed	
	kg %	kg	kg %	kg	kg %
1975	370,969(11.6)	705	1,018(3.26)	95	445(26.1)
1976	456,358(23.0)	1,856	188(0.36)	61	259(10.1)
1977	1,081,774(32.6)	7,058	226(0.58)	90	283(11.9)
1978	525,000(8.0)	2,196	122(0.27)	114	152(6.2)
1979	190,274(3.0)	1,150	65(0.09)	142	95(4.6)
1980	69,873(1.2)	883	78(0.15)	22	33(1.3)
1981	156,881(2.8)	1,226	120(0.22)	37	25(0.4)
1982	71,174(0.9)	767	65(0.14)	14	8(0.1)
1983	68,052(0.6)	632	50(0.05)	107	11(0.1)
1984	8,560,018(32.7)	11,081	72(0.12)	195	25(0.2)
1985	173,448(2.5)	757	56(0.13)	133	8(0.1)

[a]These figures only detail the amount of seizures made every year and, therefore, do not represent the quantities of illicit drugs that were destroyed as part of Mexican eradication programs.

mid-seventies, but opium seizures were unimportant (less than 1 percent each year).

Cocaine seizures (table 7) have been significant, considering that this drug is not produced in Mexico. The country has been utilized by traffickers as a transshipment route. Mexican participation in seizures was significative in the mid-seventies: 11.2 percent in 1975, 14.6 percent in 1976, and 6.8 percent in 1977 (when cocaine abuse soared in the United States). Seizures gradually descended to only 46 kg (0.2 percent) in 1981 but increased again in 1982 (3.3 percent). Although total seizures did not descend in

Table 7. Mexico: Seizures of Cocaine and Psychotropic Substances (total amounts and as percent of worldwide seizures)

Year	Cocaine kg	Psychotropic Substances units
1975	271(11.2)[a]	9,313(96.9)
1976	353(14.6)	471,083(5.9)
1977	271(6.8)	7,068,333(48.8)
1978	209(3.9)	18,744,739(82.7)
1979	95(1.1)	1,842,943(7.1)
1980	29(0.2)	10,495,584(18.7)
1981	46(0.5)	122,324(2.1)
1982	399(3.3)	323,088(1.8)
1983	324(0.8)	335,628(2.2)
1984	458(0.8)	786,085(2.8)
1985	2,562(4.5)	787,164(5.8)

[a]This value refers to kg; no units were reported.

1983 and 1984 , they represented only 0.8 percent of the worldwide amount. In 1985, however, they represented 4.5 percent of total seizures.

Finally, Mexico's seizures of psychotropic substances were very significant in some years, especially in 1975 (96.9 percent of seizures worldwide), 1977 (48.8 percent), 1978 (82.7 percent), and 1981 (20.6 percent). After 1981, seizures descended significantly but showed a trend to increase in 1984 (2.7 percent) and 1985 (5.75 percent).

It would be inappropriate to draw too many conclusions from the data and trends observed. At most, we can say that the data correlate with trends observed in other available reports. Thus, the 1975-78 period corresponded to Mexican efforts to eradicate cultivation and production which were considered highly successful. For example, the INCB affirmed in its 1980 report that a serious problem of illicit production and trafficking in opiates had emerged in Mexico. At an early stage the government recognized the problem in all its aspects, promptly elaborated a policy to deal with it, and translated that policy into specific national action. In pursuing this effort the government also cooperated closely with other countries concerned. Mexico's successful program encompassed vigorous, flexible, and innovative measures which have brought about a steep decline in the amount of opiates of Mexican origin in the international illicit traffic. In the overall bleak picture described elsewhere in this report, the action undertaken by Mexican authorities is highly commended and suggested for careful study by countries with similar problems.[8]

In 1983, apparently no increases in the Mexican supply of illicit drugs were detected. Despite a general lowering of reported seizures, the INCB again recommended the Mexican eradication programs for illicit drugs as a model for other countries:

> In determining the measures they wish to apply within their territories, the Governments of the countries concerned are advised to study the program so successfully employed by the Government of Mexico to locate and destroy illicit poppy and cannabis cultivation.[9]

---

[8]*Report of the International Narcotics Control Board for 1980,* United Nations document E/INCB/52, p. 26.
[9]*Report of the International Narcotics Control Board for 1983,* United Nations document E/INCB/1983/1, p. 32.

However, in 1985, after reports of increasing cultivation and production of illicit drugs emerged and amounts of seizures showed a new general trend to increase, the INCB stated:

> Despite the national campaign against the cultivation and traffic of illicit drugs, the Mexican Government faced an increase in the domestic production of cannabis and opium in 1984.[10]

---

[10]*Report of the International Narcotics Control Board for 1985*, United Nations document E/INCB/1985/1, p. 36.

About the Contributors

Ann J. Blanken is Acting Deputy Director, Division of Epidemiology and Statistical Analysis, National Institute on Drug Abuse (NIDA). At NIDA, she has been involved in the development of a statistical report series, the management of national data collection systems sponsored by NIDA, and the analysis of drug abuse data. She represents NIDA on several interagency committees and is actively involved in disseminating drug abuse data through consultation with government officials, researchers, and representatives of the media. She holds a B.A. degree in psychology from Duke University. Prior to joining NIDA, she worked as an analyst at the National Center for Health Statistics.

Richard B. Craig is Associate Professor of Political Science at Kent State University. He is the author of *The Bracero Program* and numerous articles and papers related to U.S.-Latin American narcopolitics. His current major interest is the impact of illicit drugs on U.S.-Mexican relations.

Samuel I. del Villar is a member of the faculty of the Centro de Estudios Internacionales at the Colegio de México. He is a former director of the periodical *Razones*, and in 1982-85, as Presidential Advisor for Special Affairs, he coordinated the elaboration of President de la Madrid's program for fighting corruption in government. He has written numerous articles on the problems posed by the drug trade for U.S.-Mexican relations.

Guadalupe González González is the coordinator of the Programa de Estudios de América del Norte at the Instituto Latinoamericano de Estudios Transnacionales and a member of the academic committee of the Bilateral Commission on the Future of United States-Mexican Relations. From 1984 to 1986 she was the director of the program of international relations studies at the Centro de Investigación y Docencia Económicas. She has written many articles on diverse aspects of Mexican foreign policy and U.S.-Mexican relations.

Rosario Green is Mexico's ambassador to the German Democratic Republic (GDR). She studied economics and international relations at the National Autonomous University of Mexico, at El Colegio de México, at Columbia University in New York, and at the Instituto para la Integración Latinoamericana (INTAL) in Buenos Aires. She has been a professor at El Colegio de México and, from 1982 to 1988, director of the Matías Romero Institute of Diplomatic Studies. Ms. Green has published ten books, including a prescient analysis of Mexico's foreign indebtedness, *El endeudamiento público externo de México: 1950-1973*, as well as *Estado y banca transnacional en México*, and, most recently, *La deuda externa de México de 1973 a 1988: de la abundancia a la escasez de créditos*. She has written articles for academic reviews and journalistic media in various languages. Ms. Green has been a consultant to the United Nations and to the Sistema Económico Latinoamericano. In 1987, she was executive director of the International Affairs Commission of the Partido Revolucionario Institucional.

Miguel Ruiz-Cabañas is a member of the Mexican Foreign Service's delegation to the United Nations and in this capacity participated in the two most recent U.N. international conferences on drug abuse and illicit drug trafficking. He completed a doctoral program in international relations at Columbia University and has written articles on international cooperation regarding the drug trade and the impact of drugs on inter-American relations.

Peter H. Smith is professor of political science and Simón Bolívar professor of Latin American studies at the University of California, San Diego. Born in Brooklyn, New York, he graduated from Harvard College in 1961 and earned a Ph.D. from Columbia University in 1966. A specialist on long-run processes of political change, Mr. Smith has written books on Argentina and on empirical methodology. His best-known work on Mexico is *Labyrinths of Power*, a study of elite recruitment and mobility. He has also co-authored a textbook entitled *Modern Latin America*. Mr. Smith has served as a department chair and academic associate dean at the University of Wisconsin and at MIT, and he is past president of the Latin American Studies Association. He was professor of history and political science at the Massachusetts Institute of Technology before joining the faculty of University of California, San Diego.